AMELIA EARHART

AMERICAN WOMEN of ACHIEVEMENT

AMELIA EARHART

NANCY SHORE

CHELSEA HOUSE PUBLISHERS

NEW YORK • PHILADELPHIA

EDITOR-IN-CHIEF: Nancy Toff
EXECUTIVE EDITOR: Remmel T. Nunn
MANAGING EDITOR: Karyn Gullen Browne
COPY CHIEF: Perry Scott King
ART DIRECTOR: Giannella Garrett
PICTURE EDITOR: Elizabeth Terhune

Staff for AMELIA EARHART:

TEXT EDITOR: Marian W. Taylor
ASSISTANT EDITOR: Maria Behan
COPYEDITORS: Gillian Bucky, Sean Dolan
DESIGN: Design Oasis
PICTURE RESEARCH: Sara Mark, Elie Porter
PRODUCTION COORDINATOR: Alma Rodriguez
COVER ILLUSTRATION: Bill Tinker

CREATIVE DIRECTOR: Harold Steinberg

5   7   9   8   6

Frontispiece courtesy of The Bettmann Archive

Library of Congress Cataloging in Publication Data

Shore, Nancy. AMELIA EARHART.

(American women of achievement)
Bibliography: p.
Includes index.
1. Earhart, Amelia, 1897–1937—Juvenile literature. 2. Air pilots—
United States—Biography—Juvenile literature. [1. Earhart, Amelia,
1897–1937. 2. Air pilots] I. Title. II. Series.
TL540.E3S48   1987   629.13'092'4 [B] [92]   86-32705

ISBN 1-55546-651-6
     0-7910-0415-5 (pbk.)

CONTENTS

"Remember the Ladies"—Matina S. Horner 7

1. Atlantic Solo 13

2. Kansas Beginnings 21

3. Wartime Hospital Worker 29

4. First Wings 37

5. Boston Social Worker 43

6. "An American Girl of the Right Image" 49

7. America's Flying Sweetheart 57

8. From the Atlantic to the Pacific 71

9. Around the World 83

10. Earhart's Legacy 101

Further Reading 106

Chronology 107

Index 108

AMERICAN WOMEN of ACHIEVEMENT

Abigail Adams
women's rights advocate

Jane Addams
social worker

Louisa May Alcott
author

Marian Anderson
singer

Susan B. Anthony
woman suffragist

Ethel Barrymore
actress

Clara Barton
*founder of the American
Red Cross*

Elizabeth Blackwell
physician

Nellie Bly
journalist

Margaret Bourke-White
photographer

Pearl Buck
author

Rachel Carson
biologist and author

Mary Cassatt
artist

Agnes De Mille
choreographer

Emily Dickinson
poet

Isadora Duncan
dancer

Amelia Earhart
aviator

Mary Baker Eddy
*founder of the Christian
Science church*

Betty Friedan
feminist

Althea Gibson
tennis champion

Emma Goldman
political activist

Helen Hayes
actress

Lillian Hellman
playwright

Katharine Hepburn
actress

Karen Horney
psychoanalyst

Anne Hutchinson
religious leader

Mahalia Jackson
gospel singer

Helen Keller
humanitarian

Jeane Kirkpatrick
diplomat

Emma Lazarus
poet

Clare Boothe Luce
author and diplomat

Barbara McClintock
biologist

Margaret Mead
anthropologist

Edna St. Vincent Millay
poet

Julia Morgan
architect

Grandma Moses
painter

Louise Nevelson
sculptor

Sandra Day O'Connor
Supreme Court justice

Georgia O'Keeffe
painter

Eleanor Roosevelt
diplomat and humanitarian

Wilma Rudolph
champion athlete

Florence Sabin
medical researcher

Beverly Sills
opera singer

Gertrude Stein
author

Gloria Steinem
feminist

Harriet Beecher Stowe
author and abolitionist

Mae West
entertainer

Edith Wharton
author

Phillis Wheatley
poet

Babe Didrikson Zaharias
champion athlete

CHELSEA HOUSE PUBLISHERS

"Remember the Ladies"

MATINA S. HORNER

Remember the Ladies." That is what Abigail Adams wrote to her husband John, then a delegate to the Continental Congress, as the Founding Fathers met in Philadelphia to form a new nation in March of 1776. "Be more generous and favorable to them than your ancestors. Do not put such unlimited power in the hands of the Husbands. If particular care and attention is not paid to the Ladies," Abigail Adams warned, "we are determined to foment a Rebellion, and will not hold ourselves bound by any Laws in which we have no voice, or Representation."

The words of Abigail Adams, one of the earliest American advocates of women's rights, were prophetic. Because when we have not "remembered the ladies," they have, by their words and deeds, reminded us so forcefully of the omission that we cannot fail to remember them. For the history of American women is as interesting and varied as the history of our nation as a whole. American women have played an integral part in founding, settling, and building our country. Some we remember as remarkable women who—against great odds—achieved distinction in the public arena: Anne Hutchinson, who in the 17th century became a charismatic religious leader; Phillis Wheatley, an 18th-century black slave who became a poet; Susan B. Anthony, whose name is synonymous with the 19th-century women's rights movement, and who led the struggle to enfranchise women; and, in our own century, Amelia Earhart, the first woman to cross the Atlantic Ocean by air.

These extraordinary women certainly merit our admiration, but other women, "common women," many of them all but forgotten, should also be recognized for their contributions to American thought and culture. Women have been community builders; they have founded schools and formed voluntary associations to help those in need; they have assumed the major responsibility for rearing children, passing on from one generation to the next the values that keep a culture alive. These and innumerable other contributions, once ignored, are now being recognized by scholars, students, and the public. It is exciting and gratifying to realize that a part of our history that was hardly acknowledged a few generations ago is now being studied and brought to light.

In recent decades, the field of women's history has grown from obscurity to a politically controversial splinter movement to academic respectability, in many cases mainstreamed into such traditional disciplines as history, economics, and psychology. Scholars of women, both female and male, have organized research centers at such prestigious institutions as Wellesley College, Stanford University, and the University of California. Other notable centers for women's studies are the Center for the American Woman and Politics at the Eagleton Institute of Politics at Rutgers University, the Henry A. Murray Research Center for the Study of Lives, at Radcliffe College, and the Women's Research and Education Institute, the research arm of the Congressional Caucus on Women's Issues. Other scholars and public figures have established archives and libraries, such as the Schlesinger Library on the History of Women in America, at Radcliffe College, and the Sophia Smith Collection, at Smith College, to collect and preserve the written and tangible legacies of women.

From the initial donation of the Women's Rights Collection in 1943, the Schlesinger Library grew to encompass vast collections documenting the manifold accomplishments of American women. Simultaneously, the women's movement in general and the academic discipline of women's studies in particular also began with a narrow definition and gradually expanded their mandate. Early causes such as woman suffrage and social reform, abolition and organized labor were joined by newer concerns such as the history of women in business and the professions and in politics and government; the study of the family; and social issues such as health policy and education.

Women, as historian Arthur M. Schlesinger, jr., once pointed out, "have constituted the most spectacular casualty of traditional history. They have made up at least half the human race, but you could never tell that by looking at the books historians write." The new breed of historians is remedying that omission. They have written books about immigrant women and about working-class women who struggled for survival in cities and about black women who met the challenges of life in rural areas. They are telling the stories of women who, despite the barriers of tradition and economics, became lawyers and doctors and public figures.

The women's studies movement has also led scholars to question traditional interpretations of their respective disciplines. For example, the study of war has traditionally been an exercise in military and political analysis, an examination of strategies planned and executed by men. But scholars of women's history have pointed out that wars have also been periods of tremendous change and even opportunity for women, because the very absence of men on the home front enabled them to expand their educational, economic, and professional activities and to assume leadership in their homes.

The early scholars of women's history showed a unique brand of courage in choosing to investigate new subjects and take new approaches to old ones. Often, like their subjects, they endured criticism and even ostracism by their academic colleagues. But their efforts have unquestionably been worthwhile, because with the publication of each new study and book another piece of the historical patchwork is sewn into place, revealing an increasingly comprehensive picture of the role of women in our rich and varied history.

Such books on groups of women are essential, but books that focus on the lives of individuals are equally indispensable. Biographies can be inspirational, offering their readers the example of people with vision who have looked outside themselves for their goals and have often struggled against great obstacles to achieve them. Marian Anderson, for instance, had to overcome racial bigotry in order to perfect her art and perform as a concert singer. Isadora Duncan defied the rules of classical dance to find true artistic freedom. Jane Addams had to break down society's notions of the proper role for women in order to create new social institutions, notably the settlement house. All of these women had to come to terms both with themselves and with the world in which they lived. Only then could they move ahead as pioneers in their chosen callings.

Biography can inspire not only by adulation but also by realism. It helps us to see not only the qualities in others that we hope to emulate, but also, perhaps, the weaknesses that made them "human." By helping us identify with the subject on a more personal level they help us to feel that we, too, can achieve such goals. We read about Eleanor Roosevelt, for instance, who occupied a unique and seemingly enviable position as the wife of the president. Yet we can sympathize with her inner dilemma: an inherently shy woman, she had to force herself to live a most public life in order to use her position to benefit others. We may not be able to imagine ourselves having the immense poetic talent of Emily Dickinson, but from her story we can understand the challenges faced by a creative woman who was expected to fulfill many family responsibilities. And though few of us will ever reach the level of athletic accomplishment displayed by Wilma Rudolph or Babe Zaharias, we can still appreciate their spirit, their overwhelming will to excel.

A biography is a multifaceted lens. It is first of all a magnification, the intimate examination of one particular life. But at the same time, it is a wide-angle lens, informing us about the world in which the subject lived. We come away from reading about one life knowing more about the social, political, and economic fabric of the time. It is for this reason, perhaps, that the great New England essayist Ralph Waldo Emerson wrote, in 1841, "There is properly no history: only biography." And it is also why biography, and particularly women's biography, will continue to fascinate writers and readers alike.

AMELIA EARHART

Amelia Earhart was called a "natural" by fellow pilots. After her first flight — a 10-minute spin over Los Angeles in 1920 — she knew her future would be in the sky. It was, she said, so "breathtakingly beautiful up there."

ONE

Atlantic Solo

At seven o'clock in the evening of May 20, 1932, a tall, slender, 34-year-old pilot wearing a baggy leather flight suit stepped calmly onto the airfield at Harbour Grace, Newfoundland. A red and gold single-engine plane stood near the hangar. Two mechanics waited patiently at its side. The pilot looked over the ocean toward the horizon, where the sun was just beginning to set. A strong wind blew in from the southwest, perfect for the takeoff.

After a few words with a friend, the pilot climbed into the cockpit of the waiting plane, started the engine, and nodded. The mechanics pulled the blocks away from the plane's wheels and it taxied to the end of the runway. Confident and elated, the pilot pointed the nose of the ship into the wind and opened the throttle. The plane picked up speed, lifted off the ground gracefully, and headed east.

Amelia Earhart had begun a daring flight that would, if successful, make her world famous as the first woman to fly across the Atlantic Ocean alone.

In the early 1930s powered flight was still relatively new. Less than three decades had passed since Orville and Wilbur Wright's famous 12-second flight in Kitty Hawk, North Carolina. Charles Lindbergh made the first solo flight across the Atlantic in 1927, but until now, no one had followed him.

The North Atlantic, unpredictable and hazardous, was known for its rapidly changing weather. Forecasters of the day could do little more than offer educated guesses based on reports from ships at sea. The difficulties of piloting a single-engine plane over thousands of miles of water were great; only an unusually courageous individual would volunteer for the physical and mental strain of such an undertaking. But Amelia Earhart was an unusual woman.

In her 12 years as an aviator, Earhart had chalked up more than 1,000 hours in the air. In 1922 she flew to a height of 14,000 feet, setting a new altitude record. In 1928, as a passenger, she became the first woman to cross the Atlantic by air. Later that year she flew from New York City to Los Angeles and back, the first woman to make a solo round trip across the United States. In 1931 she took an autogiro (an early form of helicopter) up to 18,451 feet, breaking all previous records.

The 2,000-mile Atlantic crossing would be the climax of Earhart's career thus far. It would prove to herself and others that a woman could succeed in a world where, until that time, only men had ventured.

Wanting to prepare for her flight without the presence of curious crowds or reporters, Earhart had insisted on secrecy. Very few people in the United States knew she was leaving and certainly no one in Europe expected her. To mislead the press, Earhart had sent her Lockheed Vega to Teterboro Airport in New Jersey to be overhauled by her friend Bernt Balchen, a Norwegian aviation expert and celebrated explorer. Balchen was then planning an expedition to the Antarctic, and Earhart hoped reporters would assume he planned to use her plane for his own flight to the South Pole.

While Balchen and his assistants installed a new engine and extra fuel tanks in the Vega, Earhart practiced flying "blind"—relying solely on instruments. This would be a necessary skill when she was over the ocean, where thick banks of fog often persist for miles.

By May both Earhart and the plane were ready. It was now just a matter of watching and waiting for the right weather. On the morning of May 19, Earhart was discussing last-minute details with Balchen at Teterboro when her husband, George Putnam, called from New York. Putnam, who had been consulting with weather expert Dr. James "Doc"

Kimball, reported that conditions were now right for takeoff.

That settled it. Earhart and Balchen took off for Newfoundland, Balchen piloting the plane while Earhart rested. Detailed reports from George Putnam awaited them in Harbour Grace. "Outlook not perfect, but promising," he had cabled. "Go ahead." Deciding on an early-evening departure, Earhart left Balchen and the mechanics to refuel and give the engine a last-minute tune-up while she went off to take a final nap. She was going to need all the rest she could get.

At 7:12 that evening she was airborne. The adventure of a lifetime had begun. The little plane moved across a calm sky in which vast fields of clouds glowed orange in the slanting rays of the lingering sun. At 8:30 Earhart made the first entry in her logbook: "Two icebergs." An hour later the sun began to fall below the horizon and the moon rose over a low bank of clouds. Flying at about 12,000 feet, Earhart settled back in the tiny cockpit. She was wide awake and excited. Ever since her first "hop" in 1920 in a Los Angeles aviation-school plane, flying had been the most important thing in her life.

"Beauty and adventure have a certain value of their own which can be weighed only in spiritual scales," she was to write later.

Suddenly, glancing at the instrument panel, Earhart was shocked to see that the altimeter (the instrument that records height above the ground) had failed. Its needle swung crazily around the dial. To her dismay, she realized it would be useless for the rest of the flight.

A moment later the moon disappeared

Charles Lindbergh flies The Spirit of St. Louis *over Paris, the termination point of his 1927 transatlantic flight. Known as "The Lone Eagle," Lindbergh was the first person to fly solo across the Atlantic.*

behind a bank of clouds and a violent thunderstorm began. Strong winds and heavy rain buffeted the tiny ship. Hoping to climb above the storm, Earhart nosed the plane upward. It immediately began to lose speed; ice was forming on the wings. The temperature in the plane was bitter cold, and the tachometer (the instrument that indicates the number of engine revolutions per minute) had frozen.

Knowing she had to get into warmer air, Earhart put the plane into a spin. The plane's barograph (the instrument that indicates barometric pressure) showed a drop of 3,000 feet—straight down. When Earhart saw the waves breaking on the surface of the water beneath her, she hurriedly pulled the plane level.

With the altimeter broken and the fog swirling around the ship, she could not tell if she was 10 feet or 100 feet above the ocean. There was nothing left to do but seek a middle ground, somewhere between the ocean and the icy upper air.

At about 11:30 she felt a slight shudder in the plane. At the same moment she saw flames coming through a broken weld in the engine's exhaust outlet. She knew that if the section separated, the subsequent vibration would tear the plane apart. She reasoned, however, that the metal was very heavy and would probably last until she reached land. If she turned back she might have difficulty getting to Newfoundland. And landing with a heavy load of fuel would be dangerous; she might wind up in a ball of fire. Earhart made her decision. "I'd much prefer drowning to burning up," she later recalled thinking. She continued resolutely on her eastward course.

The foul weather kept up. And Earhart, as she said later, continued "just plowing through the soup and not looking out of the cockpit again until morning came." When the water seemed too close she nosed back upward. When the wings iced up she headed down to the warmer air below.

As dawn broke over the Atlantic, Earhart found herself flying over a layer of "little fluffy white clouds that grew packed until they resembled a vast snow-

About to break an altitude record, Earhart waves from the cockpit of an autogiro in 1931. She took the aircraft — an early version of today's helicopter — to a height of 15,000 feet, later breaking her own record by flying to 18,415 feet.

16

Earhart gets an approving grin from Bernt Balchen, the Norwegian aviator who acted as consultant for her 1932 transatlantic flight. When she asked him if he thought she could make it, he answered in two words: "You bet."

field." The storm had lifted at last. Now, however, the glare of the sun on the "snowfield" was almost blinding. The weary pilot guided her ship under the clouds.

Tense and exhausted from her struggle to keep the plane on course through the night, Earhart punched a hole in a can of tomato juice and sipped. Her fingers, gripped tightly around the controls, were beginning to ache.

The last two hours of the flight were the most difficult. The weld had all but burned through and the plane was vibrating badly. More trouble: a faulty gauge in the reserve gas tank; gasoline began to leak into the cockpit. Earhart's main objective was to reach land as quickly as possible and come down in the nearest place, wherever that was. Finally she sighted a small fishing vessel and knew she was nearing the Irish coast. A wave of relief surged through her. It had been the longest and loneliest night of her life.

Looking for a spot to land, she followed a railroad track that would, she hoped, lead her to a city with an airfield. Finding none, she brought the plane down in a meadow near Londonderry, "frightening all the cows in the country" in the process. In 15 hours and 18 minutes she had crossed the vast Atlantic. She had done it alone, and she had done it faster than anyone on record.

When she climbed stiffly out of the cockpit, she saw a farmer gaping at her in disbelief. She removed her leather flying helmet and shook out her tousled, reddish-blond hair. "Hi," she said brightly. "I've come from America." "Have you now?" he replied skeptically.

In Londonderry the British press caught wind of the news. The story of

Earhart's Lockheed Vega, fitted with extra fuel tanks and a new engine before her 1932 Newfoundland-to-Ireland "hop," had a cruising range of 3,200 miles.

Earhart's daring transatlantic flight was quickly flashed around the world. Britain's King George V cabled the royal family's congratulations. From London, Lady Nancy Astor, the first woman elected to the British Parliament, wired, "Come to us and I'll lend you a nightgown." Andrew Mellon, the American ambassador to Great Britain, invited Earhart to stay at the U.S. Embassy. Paramount News sent a plane to Ireland to fly her to England. (Paramount was one of the companies that produced newsreels, short films presenting current events, which were shown in movie theaters in the days before television.)

Earhart was lauded by the press and showered with international honors and awards. When she returned (on an ocean liner) to the United States, President Herbert Hoover invited her to the White House, where he presented her with a gold medal from the National Geographic Society. Earhart's acceptance speech was characteristically modest. "I hope the flight has meant something to women in aviation," she said. "If it has I shall feel justified. I can't claim anything else."

Orville Wright, 65, meets Earhart, 39, at a Philadelphia aeronautical exhibit in 1936. Wright had made the world's first powered flight — remaining aloft for 12 seconds — at Kitty Hawk, North Carolina, in 1903.

Cheering well-wishers surround Earhart and her Vega in Londonderry, Ireland. People all over the world were excited by the news that a lone woman had crossed the vast Atlantic Ocean by air.

Six-year-old Amelia Earhart holds hands with her little sister Muriel on the porch of their grandparents' home in Atchison, Kansas. Sedate neighbors were sometimes shocked by the antics of the unconventional Earhart girls.

T W O

Kansas Beginnings

Whenever anyone asks me about my work in aviation," wrote Amelia Earhart in 1932, "I know that sooner or later I shall hear, 'And of course you were mechanical when you were a girl, weren't you?' As a matter of fact, in a small way I was— witness the trap I made to catch the chickens that strayed into our yard. My girlhood was much like that of many another American girl who was growing up at the time I was, with just the kind of fun and good times we all had back then."

Amelia Earhart was born in the Atchison, Kansas, home of her maternal grandparents, Alfred and Amelia Otis, on July 24, 1897. A descendant of American Revolutionary statesman James Otis, Judge Otis had left New York State in 1854 to settle in Atchison. In 1862 he went back east, married Amelia Harres of Philadelphia, and brought her to Atchison. Traveling to Kansas by train and steamboat, the new Mrs. Otis saw a frontier landscape. Buffalo bones lined the railroad tracks and Indians made up a large part of the population.

By 1900 Atchison had become an important railroad center. "There were no Indians around when I arrived," Amelia Earhart lamented later, "though I hoped for many a day some would turn up. And the nearest I got to buffalos was the discovery of an old fur robe rotting away in the barn."

Judge Otis built a handsome brick house on a bluff above the Missouri River; there the young couple settled down to raise a family. Otis divided his time between the U.S. District Court and his duties as president of the Atchison Savings Bank. His wife attended afternoon teas, paid social calls, and brought up her children. There were eight; Amelia's mother Amy was the fourth child.

Amy Otis, a fine horsewoman and a good dancer, was a popular member of young Atchison society. Intelligent and cultured, she often spent evenings discussing politics with her father's friends. After a long illness, she decided against college; instead she spent much of her time accompanying her father on his frequent western business trips. In 1890 she climbed Pike's Peak in the Colorado Rocky Mountains, becoming the first

Amy and Edwin Earhart were unusually liberal parents for their day. They allowed their tomboy daughters, Amelia and Muriel, to wear trousers and play such "unfeminine" games as baseball.

woman to reach its 14,000-foot summit.

Amy was expected to make a sensible marriage, choosing a wealthy and ambitious man who could give her the kind of home she was used to. Love, however, is not always practical. At her "coming out" ball in 1890, one of Amy's brothers introduced her to Edwin Earhart, his college roommate. Earhart was a good-looking but impoverished law student at the University of Kansas. He and Amy danced the night away; they were soon engaged, much to the chagrin of the formidable judge. He told young Edwin he would not be considered a suitable husband for Amy unless he could earn at least $50 a month.

Edwin Earhart, the youngest of David and Mary Earhart's 12 children, had been born near Atchison. The senior Earhart was a farmer, teacher, and Evangelical Lutheran missionary. He and his wife worked long hours, battling crop failure, drought, dust storms, and locusts in their effort to wrest a living from the tough Kansas sod.

On weekdays David Earhart taught school; on Sundays he preached to a congregation of Indians and settlers. His great hope was that his youngest son would become a clergyman, but Edwin chose the law instead. He worked his way through school by doing odd jobs and tutoring his fellow students. Edwin Earhart was a charming young man, imaginative and witty, a lover of books and music. Amy Otis fell in love with him immediately.

Following his graduation from law school in 1894, Edwin Earhart got a job settling insurance claims for a midwestern railroad. His salary met Judge Otis's requirements, and Amy Otis received permission to marry him. After their 1895 wedding, the young couple moved into a house in Kansas City, bought and furnished by the bride's father. Judge Otis urged his son-in-law to open a private legal practice in Atchison, but the adventurous Edwin preferred his railroad job, which kept him on the road most of the time.

Amy Earhart was deeply in love with her young husband, but the long periods of loneliness and the sudden transition from pampered debutante to middleclass wife were hard on her. After the stillbirth of her first baby, she moved back to her parents' home in Atchison. Here she gave birth to a daughter, Amelia Mary, named for her two grandmothers.

Not long after Amelia's arrival, the Earharts had another daughter, Muriel. Amy Earhart often joined her husband on business trips now, leaving her two little girls with her own parents. Perched above the wide Missouri, the big, sprawling Otis house and its spacious grounds were a fine setting for fun and adventure. Hand in hand, Amelia and Muriel would race along the paths leading down to the river, searching for arrowheads, playing pioneers and Indians.

To the delight of her sister and friends, one of Amelia's early projects was a makeshift roller coaster. Working with the quiet determination that was to become

Judge Alfred Otis built this Atchison, Kansas, house for his wife Amelia in the 1860s. Born here were the Otises' eight children as well as their granddaughters Amelia and Muriel Earhart.

Their grandmother may have enjoyed rolling her hoop, but the Earhart girls preferred livelier games. Here, Muriel climbs ropes while Amelia tries out her new homemade stilts.

her hallmark, Amelia used fence rails to build tracks leading down the steep slope of a shed roof to the ground. The cart was a plank attached to old roller-skate wheels. On Amelia's first test of her invention, she careened down the roof, screaming "It's just like flying!"—and crashed straight into the ground.

Breathless but undaunted, she ran to the barn for lumber to extend the track along the ground. The redesigned roller coaster was a great success until it was noticed by the girls' grandparents. Announcing firmly that such rough play was not for young ladies, they removed the offending contraption.

One day, when Amelia hopped over the garden fence on her way home from school, Grandmother Otis scolded her. The most daring thing *she* ever did as a young girl, she said, was roll her hoop around the public square. Edwin and

Amelia (center) and Muriel (left) visit their grandparents in Atchison in 1908. At right are the girls' parents, Amy and Edwin Earhart.

Amy Earhart, however, held liberal views about child-rearing. They encouraged their daughters to develop their bodies and minds to the best of their abilities. Much to the dismay of Grandmother Otis, the girls' activities included baseball, fishing, and roaming the woods and fields.

"Dear Dad, Muriel and I would like footballs this year, please. We need them especially as we have plenty of baseballs and bats," Amelia wrote one year. Christmas came and so did the footballs.

To accommodate her daughters' active lifestyles, Amy Earhart allowed them to wear bloomers, loose-fitting trousers that were just beginning to come into vogue. Amelia and Muriel raced around unhampered while the other local girls walked sedately in their traditional long dresses. "We were comfortable, unconventional, and entirely happy tomboys," wrote Muriel later.

When the children of Atchison went sledding, most of the girls sat primly upright while they coasted down slopes on sleds with wooden runners. Edwin Earhart, however, bought boys' sleds with steel runners for his daughters. One day, flat on her stomach as she hurtled down a steep hill near the house, Amelia caught sight of a horse and buggy on her path below. She shouted to the driver, but he did not hear her. As she would do many times in later life, Amelia swiftly chose a course of action and followed through on it.

Aiming her sled between the front and hind legs of the horse, she closed her eyes and shot down the hill. She streaked safely under the horse—no doubt leaving the startled driver to wonder what young ladies were coming to these days.

"Unfortunately I lived at a time when girls were still girls," Earhart wrote later, in *The Fun of It.* "I was fond of basketball, bicycling, and tennis, and I tried any and all strenuous games. . . . With the intense pleasure exercise gave me, I might have attained more skill and more grace than I did. As it was, I just played exultingly, and built up all kinds of wrong habits."

"Amelia was more fun to play with than anyone else," observed one of her cousins later. "I admired her ability, stood in awe of her information and intelligence, adored her imagination, and loved her for herself."

To expand their daughters' horizons, the Earharts would sometimes bend their own rules, allowing them, for example to stay up past their bedtime to watch an eclipse of the moon. In 1910 the whole family gathered on a neighbor's roof to see Halley's comet, a celestial phenomenon visible only once every 75 years.

Edwin Earhart had a lively imagination and a quick sense of humor. He entertained his daughters with exciting adventure stories that sometimes ran for weeks. The stories burgeoned into real-life games on Saturdays, when he often came home from work early to play "cowboys and Indians" with Amelia, Muriel, and their friends.

In 1908 Edwin Earhart was promoted to a better job with the railroad and moved his family to Des Moines, Iowa.

When Amelia was 11 years old, she went to the Iowa State Fair; there she saw her first airplane. "It was a thing of rusty wire and wood and looked not at all interesting," she wrote later. "One of the grownups pointed it out to me and said, 'Look, dear, it flies.' I looked as directed but confess I was much more interested in an absurd hat made of an inverted peachbasket which I had just purchased for fifteen cents."

The carefree, happy-go-lucky existence that Amelia had known since birth was not to last. Edwin Earhart now had more money and greater prestige, but he was not happy. He had liked life on the road, and office routine bored him. He did, however, enjoy the company of his hard-drinking co-workers; here were men who treated him with a warmth and respect he had never received from the high-minded Otises. When his new friends invited him to join them on drinking bouts, he accepted eagerly—and often.

As his drinking increased, his job performance deteriorated. Eventually, "Dad's sickness," as the girls referred to their father's alcoholism, went out of control. He was fired by the railroad. With their father alternately abusive and morose, Amelia and Muriel were by turns pitying, miserable, and embarrassed.

To make matters worse, their grandmother Otis, who had been aware of Edwin Earhart's "sickness," died in 1911. Her will directed that Amy Earhart's share of the family fortune be put into trust for 20 years—or until her son-in-law's death.

For Edwin Earhart, this slap in the face was anything but sobering; his drinking and mistreatment of his family increased.

Earhart was 17 when this picture was made in St. Paul, Minnesota. Because Edwin Earhart's alcoholism made it hard for him to keep a job, his family moved often. They lived in St. Paul from 1913 to 1914.

The Earharts now began a series of yearly moves; as Edwin Earhart found and lost jobs from Minnesota to Missouri, the girls went from one school to another.

Finally, old friends invited Amy Earhart and her daughters to live with them in Chicago. There they settled temporarily, financially destitute and emotionally drained. Edwin Earhart moved in with his sister in Kansas City, where he opened a law office.

"I know that the hardship and mental suffering that Amelia and I endured as adolescents made an indelible impression on us and help to explain some of Amelia's actions and attitudes later in life," wrote her sister Muriel later in *Courage Is the Price*.

Whatever her misery over her parents' separation, Amelia did not allow it to quench her spirit. On the contrary, she threw herself into her schoolwork with renewed vigor. She had become interested in chemistry, and after inspecting the laboratories of several Chicago high schools, she decided to enter Hyde Park High. Wholly engaged in her studies, she was also completely indifferent to grades and scholarship awards. It was the work that mattered to her.

One of her teachers explained that Amelia never won prizes because she refused to document the steps she used to work out mathematical problems. Amelia said, "I don't care especially about the prize. I know that I know how to get the answers and Miss Walton knows I know. So what's the difference who has the medal?"

Amelia developed a reputation for ec-

Students at Chicago's Hyde Park High School salute one of their most famous alumni: Amelia Earhart, class of 1915. On this visit, 17 years after her graduation, Earhart finally collected her high school diploma.

centricity and aloofness among her fellow students. "I don't think that boys particularly cared for me," she wrote later, "but I can't remember being very sad about the situation." She did not show up for her graduation ceremony and did not get her diploma until 1932 (when, at a civic reception in her honor, the mayor of Chicago smilingly presented it to her). The caption under her picture in the 1915 Hyde Park High School yearbook read, "The girl in brown who walks alone."

Although Earhart wears a graduate's cap and gown in her 1917 Ogontz School yearbook picture, she never graduated from the "female college." She left school early to nurse wounded war veterans in a Canadian hospital.

THREE

Wartime Hospital Worker

After Amelia Earhart graduated from high school in 1915, she and her mother and sister went to Kansas City, where her father had set up an independent law practice. He seemed, for the time being at least, to have his alcoholism under control. Because his small income offered meager prospects for the girls' future, he persuaded his wife to go to court and contest her mother's will.

Amy Earhart won a settlement of $60,000 and immediately decided to send her daughters to college. Muriel chose St. Margaret's in Toronto, Canada, and Amelia enrolled in the Ogontz School, a two-year "female college" near Philadelphia.

Ogontz was a conservative school that emphasized art and literature as well as "proper behavior" for its students. Its classes in old-fashioned etiquette greatly amused the independent and unconventional Amelia Earhart. An early note to her mother—quoted in Earhart biographer Jean Backus's *Letters from Amelia*—records her reaction to one of these lessons.

"You will 'pop' when I tell you about a drawing-room evening we had last Thursday. 'Miss Pughsey's evening' they call it. She had us walk, bow, sit, shake hands, etc., etc.... The funniest thing was the sitting. She put a little chair in the middle of this huge room and we all aimed at it and tried to clamber on it gracefully. It was a scream. One of the girls landed with her legs crossed on the extreme edge. I got on but not with noticeable grace as there was no comment made."

Now 19 years old, Earhart was slender, intense, and studious. Her days were filled with lectures, visits to the opera, tennis, horseback riding, and art classes. Although she had joined a sorority when she arrived at Ogontz, she soon became an opponent of these exclusive social clubs. She also campaigned for intellectual freedom in literary discussions. Accused of atheism (disbelief in God) when she defended a famous Hindu poet's right to worship as he believed, she replied, "God, to me, is a power that helps me to be good. The way we worship isn't a bit important."

Ogontz's headmistress, Abby Sutherland, later wrote, "Amelia was always pushing into unknown seas in her reading. The look in her straightforward, eager eyes was most fascinating in those days. Her style of dressing was always simple and becoming. At that period her purse, as well as her innate taste, required the fewest and simplest clothes. But she helped very much to impress the over-indulged girls with the beauty and comfort of simple dressing."

Almost all of Earhart's fellow students viewed education for women as a stepping stone to marriage, but she thought of it as preparation for a career. Increasingly interested in the changing role of women, she began to keep a scrapbook of clippings about women's achievements in fields traditionally dominated by men. Entries included "Mrs. Paul Bund, fire lookout at Harney Peak, South Dakota," "Mrs. Mithram Tata of Bombay, first Indian woman admitted to the bar," "Mrs. E. E. Abernathy, Oklahoma's only female bank president."

When Earhart added volunteer work for the local Red Cross to her schoolwork and her duties as vice president of the senior class, her mother wrote the headmistress a concerned note. In a letter to her "Dear Mammy," Earhart protested, "Don't write Miss S. letters of advice and warning. They go through the whole faculty and come to me and I just shrivel. I am not overdoing and all that is needed to bouncing health is plenty to eat and happiness. Consider me bursting, please."

In 1917 Earhart went to Toronto to spend Christmas with her sister. The United States had entered World War I the previous spring. Canadian troops had been fighting in Europe since 1914, but,

Campaigning for women's right to vote, demonstrators prepare for a 1918 parade. Earhart was not directly involved in the suffragist movement, but she fought for the equality of the sexes all her life.

sequestered at Ogontz, Earhart had not yet confronted the war's brutal realities. She was shocked by the sight of the wounded soldiers she encountered in Canada.

"There for the first time I realized what world war meant," she wrote later. "Instead of new uniforms and brass bands I saw only the results of four years' desperate struggle; men without arms and legs, men who were paralyzed and men who were blind. One day I saw four one-legged men at once, walking as best they could down the street together."

In a letter to her mother she said, "I'd like to stay here and help in the hospitals. I can't bear the thought of going back to school and being so useless." After Christmas she returned to Philadelphia to finish her senior term, but her heart was no longer in her studies. Life at school suddenly seemed frivolous and unimportant.

By February she had persuaded her reluctant mother to allow her to leave without graduating. Packing up her few belongings, she returned to Toronto to nurse the war-wounded. She bequeathed Ogontz the motto she had composed for the class of 1918: "Honor is the foundation of courage."

After taking a course in Red Cross first aid, Earhart was assigned to Toronto's Spadina Military Hospital as a nurse's aide. On duty 10 hours a day, she did everything from scrubbing floors and washing trays to giving back rubs. Tireless and cheerful, "Sister Amelia" soon became a favorite with the sick and discouraged men. She played the piano for them and, assigned to work in the hospital kitchen, did her best to upgrade the dreary monotony of the hospital meals.

When she was not working, Earhart played tennis, went horseback riding with her sister, and cultivated friendships with hospital patients, many of whom were British and French pilots. One afternoon, when she and a friend were visiting a local airfield, one of the pilots decided it might be amusing to give the young women a scare. He put his plane into a dive, aiming straight at them. While her

American soldiers depart for the front during World War I. Although the United States had entered the war in April 1917, Earhart was not fully aware of its horrors until December, when she encountered wounded soldiers in Canada.

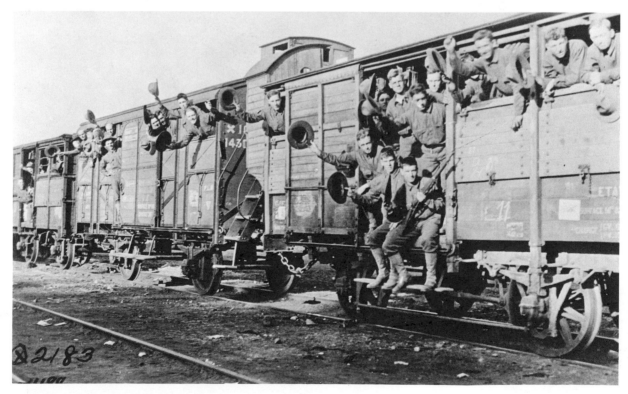

Nurse's aide Earhart takes a break from her duties at Spadina Military Hospital in Toronto, Canada, in 1918. Known as "Sister Amelia," the energetic and popular young volunteer worked regular 10-hour shifts.

friend dashed for safety, Earhart stayed where she was, mesmerized.

In Earhart's book *Last Flight*, she recalled the "mingled fear and pleasure which surged over me as I watched that small plane at the top of its earthward swoop. Common sense told me if something went wrong with the mechanism, or if the pilot lost control, he, the airplane, and I would be rolled up in a ball to-

gether. I did not understand it at the time but I believe that little red airplane said something to me as it swished by." According to Earhart, "I determined then that I would some day ride one of these devil machines."

From then on, Earhart began to spend what spare time she had at Armour Heights, a military training ground near Toronto, watching the planes take off and land and talking to the young pilots about flying.

Earhart's experience in Toronto left her with a deep interest in medicine and a passionate opposition to war. The memory of useless agony and wasted youth was fixed in her mind forever. Surely, she thought, there must be a way to ease hostilities between countries, to bring people closer together, and to promote understanding. In 1918 aviation was nothing more than a casual interest for Earhart. Another decade would pass before she began to see a connection between her dream of world peace and the winged ships of the air.

Earhart was still in Toronto when the war ended in November 1918. During the influenza epidemic that followed, she continued to work in the hospital, "helping," as she put it, "to ladle out medicine from buckets" in the overcrowded wards.

Eventually, the long hours of hard work among the sick and dying took their toll on "Sister Amelia"; the nurse became a patient. She found herself with an aggravated case of sinusitis, an inflammation of the nasal passages that would plague her for the rest of her life.

In our own time, Earhart's ailment would be treated with antibiotics, but such remedies were unknown then. Doctors treated sinusitis by flushing out, or irrigating, the sinus cavities. Earhart referred to these extremely uncomfortable treatments as "washings out."

Earhart spent the spring of 1919 recovering from her attack of sinusitis. She and her mother went to stay in Northampton, Massachusetts, where Muriel was enrolled at Smith College. As soon as she was well enough, Earhart signed up for a class in automobile-engine repair at Smith; what she learned there about mo-

tor-driven vehicles would prove unexpectedly useful in days to come.

When school was out, the three women went to Lake George, a vacation spot in New York state. Earhart continued to suffer from severe sinus headaches, but her health was noticeably improved after a summer of energetic swimming and boating.

While they were at Lake George, they got a letter from Edwin Earhart, who had moved from Kansas City to Los Angeles. He said that he was now a member of the

Serving food to children whose families have been stricken by influenza during the epidemic of 1918, volunteers wear protective gauze masks. Earhart worked in a Toronto hospital during the epidemic, which killed 15 million people around the world.

Red-blond tresses streaming from her bathing cap, Earhart prepares for a swim in 1919. After she learned to fly, the aviator always wore her hair cut short.

Church of Christian Science, that he had conquered his alcoholism, and that he wanted his wife to return to him. Amy Earhart was willing to try again, but first she wanted to settle her daughter Amelia at Columbia University, where she had enrolled as a premedical student.

Amy and Amelia Earhart went to New York City in the fall of 1919. After her mother left, Earhart signed up for a heavy load of classes. "The courses she was taking," a friend later reported, "were really a three-man job, with a full quota of lectures and lab courses at Columbia, and another full quota at Barnard [the women's college affiliated with Columbia]. Apparently Columbia and Barnard didn't compare notes, as she wouldn't have been permitted to carry a load like that if anyone had known." Now 22, Earhart was clearly trying to make up for lost time.

New York City—especially when compared to suburban Philadelphia—was a feast of social and intellectual nourishment. Earhart had almost no spending money, but she attended innumerable free public lectures, concerts, and poetry readings. When she took time off from studying and absorbing culture, she went hiking with friends.

Reminiscing about Earhart's time at Columbia, a friend wrote, "Amelia found out how to get the key to the roof of the university library at Columbia. And more than once we climbed the endless steps, and up over the roof on our hands and knees to the very top of the dome. There we found the freedom of the skies, a world which was secret from our professors."

Earhart was enjoying her life in New York, and she was still intrigued with the study of medicine. She began to realize, however, that she was more excited by theory than by practice, and she decided to become a medical researcher rather than a doctor.

The summer of 1920 presented problems that seemed more pressing than education: Amy and Edwin Earhart, now reunited in Los Angeles, wrote to their older daughter, urging her to come and live with them. She could, they pointed out, finish her studies on the West Coast. Earhart's family loyalty was strong, and she obediently headed west. She planned to spend the summer with her parents, doing everything she could to help patch up the marriage. Before she left New York, she told her sister she would return in the fall. "I'm going to come back here," insisted Earhart, "and live my own life."

A few weeks later, at an airfield near Los Angeles, Amelia Earhart was to have an experience that would change her life forever.

Earhart relaxes at Lake George, New York, where she went to recover from an attack of chronic sinusitis (inflammation of the nasal passages) in 1919.

Once she committed herself to aviation, Earhart dressed for the role. Her standard "uniform" included a leather jacket, flying helmet, and goggles.

FOUR

First Wings

There are two kinds of stones," Amelia Earhart once wrote, "one of which rolls. Because I selected a father who was a railroad man it has been my fortune to roll."

In the summer of 1920, Earhart "rolled" out to the West Coast and into her parents' large Los Angeles house. The senior Earharts were supplementing their income by renting out rooms, one of them to Samuel Chapman, a young chemical engineer from Massachusetts. Chapman was immediately drawn to Earhart's ready wit and level, gray-eyed gaze. The attraction was mutual, and the pair soon began to spend their leisure hours together.

Earhart was also attracted to southern California and its wide variety of outdoor sports. She was, as she later said, "fond of automobiles, tennis, horseback riding, and almost anything that is active and carried out in the open." She and Chapman swam and played tennis, attended plays and political meetings together, and spent long hours talking about books and world affairs. Amy and Edwin Earhart liked Sam Chapman; they assumed that

their daughter would marry him and become a conventional, contented housewife. They did not, it seems, know her as well as they thought.

The leisure-time activity Earhart enjoyed most was not one she shared with Chapman. She had never forgotten the excitement she had experienced at the flying field in Toronto, and now she found herself irresistibly drawn to the airfields that had sprung up around Los Angeles.

In 1920 aviation was still something of a novelty. Airshows were a popular pastime; on weekends crowds jammed the airfields to watch retired army pilots "stunt" in old warplanes. Earhart went to her first air meet—where the sky, she later recalled, "was a perfect blue"—with her father. Entranced by the sight of the little planes soaring and diving through the air, she asked her father to inquire about the price of flying lessons. He returned with a discouraging report: local pilots charged $1,000 to teach a student to fly. For the Earharts, scraping along on what was left of the Otis legacy, it was an impossible sum.

Amelia Earhart, however, was not easily daunted. She wanted to fly, and fly she would. A few days later she paid a professional pilot $1 for a 10-minute ride over Hollywood. From that moment on, she was committed to the air. "By the time I had gotten two or three hundred feet off the ground," she wrote later, "I knew I had to fly."

In *Letters from Amelia*, Jean Backus writes, "Nothing had prepared [Earhart] for the physical and emotional impact of flight. No other urge, no intellectual, sexual, or social excitement ever involved or moved her as totally as soaring into the subtle environment where her most secret self was free of earthly concerns and subject to no human influence but her own. Here was the ultimate happiness."

"I think I'd like to learn to fly," Amelia announced casually that night at dinner with her parents.

Her father, perhaps assuming his daughter was voicing a passing fancy, responded just as casually. "Not a bad idea," he said. "When do you start?"

She started at once. As a first step, she signed up for lessons on credit. She was confident that somehow or other the bill would be paid, but her father was dismayed. Faced with the reality of the lessons, he told her he simply could not afford them.

"Evidently he thought that if he didn't pay I wouldn't fly," Earhart wrote later, "but I was determined." To finance the lessons, she got her first paying job, sorting mail for the telephone company in Los Angeles. From then on, she later recalled, "the family scarcely saw me. I worked all week and spent what I had of Saturday and Sunday at the airport."

The airfield was on the outskirts of town; to get there meant an hour's streetcar ride followed by a walk of several miles along a dusty highway. In those early days of aviation, serious fliers dressed the part in semimilitary outfits. Wanting to be as inconspicuous as possible in an arena dominated by men, Earhart cropped her hair and donned breeches, boots, and a man's leather jacket. She reveled in the romantic at-

Earhart models her "working girl" outfit in her parents' Los Angeles backyard in 1920. To pay for flying lessons, she took a job at the local telephone company, but she spent every spare minute at the airfield.

mosphere of the makeshift airfield with its ramshackle hangars and secondhand planes.

Her flight instructor was Neta Snook, a fine pilot and the first woman to graduate from the prestigious Curtiss School of Aviation. Snook insisted that her eager pupil learn the name and function of every part of the training plane before going aloft. The trainer, a Curtiss Canuck biplane, had dual controls, a safety device that enabled an instructor to override decisions made by a student in the air. With Snook in the rear cockpit, Earhart practiced takeoffs and landings. When Snook was satisfied that her student had mastered these basics, she began to teach her various aerial maneuvers and stunt-flying techniques.

A thorough knowledge of "stunting" is essential to pilots; it prepares them to cope with any emergency that may arise in flight. "The fundamental stunts are slips, stalls, spins, loops, barrels, and rolls," explained Earhart in her book *Last Flight*. "Unless a pilot has actually recovered from a stall, has actually put his plane into a spin and brought it out, he cannot know accurately what these acts entail."

Earhart spent as much time as she could with the other pilots at the airfield. Trying to learn everything there was to know about aviation, she asked innumerable questions and listened avidly as the experienced fliers talked "shop." She already knew a fair amount about motors from her class in automobile repair, but she knew she needed to learn much more. These pilots, most of whom had flown during World War I, had picked up their techniques the hard way. They were

Ready for a lesson, flying instructor Neta Snook (left) and student Amelia Earhart prepare to board a Kinner Airster biplane at a Los Angeles airport in 1920.

experts at night flying, staying on course over unfamiliar territory, changing direction or speed quickly.

The veteran pilots found Earhart good-natured, unpretentious, and quick to learn. She would crawl under a plane, make repairs, and, covered with grease, emerge smiling happily. She was, concluded the airfield crowd, "a natural."

At last the time came for her to solo. She went up 5,000 feet and, as she put it, "played around a little and came back." Although she made a less than perfect landing, she was thrilled. "It's so breathtakingly beautiful up there," she said. "I want to fly whenever I can." And she wanted a plane of her own. She started saving money, willing to forego all luxuries until she could afford her heart's desire.

Her first solo flight behind her, Earhart signed up for advanced flying lessons. She went to work in a photography studio to pay for them. Later she was to write, "I've had 28 different jobs in my life and I hope I'll have 28 more. Experiment! Meet new people. That's better than any college education. By adventuring about, you become accustomed to the unexpected. The unexpected then becomes what it really is—the inevitable."

Flying, which had begun as a casual interest, was rapidly developing into an obsession for Earhart. Her father considered the pastime dangerous and foolish, but her mother was enthusiastic, even after her daughter had made two crash landings. The first time, a rainstorm had forced her down in a farmer's meadow, leaving her suspended upside down by her safety belt. Flung from the cockpit

during her second forced landing, this one in a weedy field, she again emerged unhurt. Amy Earhart was calm in both cases. She said that when her daughter did things, "she always did them very carefully. . . . She thought it out and her mind was quick and I had no special anxiety."

By 1922 Earhart had given up her plans to return to college. She continued to spend much of her free time with Sam Chapman, and her parents still assumed the pair would marry. Marriage, however, was not on Earhart's list of priorities. That

A proud Earhart shows off the present — a second-hand Kinner Canary — she gave herself for her 25th birthday. She bought the bright yellow plane with financial help from her mother and sister.

summer she received a pilot's license from the Fédération Aéronautique Internationale, the only agency that issued licenses at the time. She was now one of the few women in the world licensed to fly.

On July 24, 1922, Amelia Earhart was 25 years old; her birthday present—paid for with her own savings and generous contributions from her mother and sister—was an airplane, a bright yellow Kinner Canary. It was secondhand, and its single, 60-horsepower engine sent rough vibrations through its cockpit, but Earhart thought it was wonderful. "Immediately," she wrote, "I found that my whole feeling of flying changed." In exchange for free hangar space, she worked for aircraft manufacturer W.G. Kinner, demonstrating the plane to prospective buyers.

Edwin Earhart and his two daughters attended an air meet at Los Angeles's Rogers Field in October 1922. As he and his younger daughter anxiously scanned the sky, his older daughter rapidly disappeared from view, soaring aloft in her Kinner Canary. When the small yellow plane landed an hour later, the airfield's loudspeakers boomed out the news: Amelia Earhart had climbed to a height of 14,000 feet, breaking the women's altitude record.

That record was soon overtaken by well-known aviator Ruth Nichols; it is nonetheless memorable for being the earliest of Earhart's many aviation "firsts." She made an effort to break the new record a few weeks later. Taking her plane up to 12,000 feet, she ran into a dense bank of clouds; with snow stinging her

Earhart's pilot's license, issued by the Fédération Aéronautique Internationale in 1922, shows her in a leather helmet. The FAI represented fliers in both Europe and the United States.

face as she sat in the Canary's open cockpit, she found herself flying blind through an airy limbo. Undaunted, she continued to climb. When the snow turned to sleet, however, she knew it was time to abandon the effort, at least for the moment. She kicked the rudder and sent the plane into a downward spin. Zooming through the fog, she leveled off at 3,000 feet and landed safely.

"What the hell were you trying to do?" shouted another pilot. "If the fog had closed in completely all the way down to the ground we would have had to dig you out in pieces!"

"I suppose you would have," said Earhart coolly. She was, in fact, thoroughly shaken by the harrowing flight, but she had no intention of letting any of the men on the field know it.

*Earhart prepares to take off from a Boston airport in 1926. Flying in open cockpits —
standard in the aircraft of the time — was hard on pilots who suffered, as Earhart did,
from sinus problems.*

FIVE

Boston Social Worker

In the summer of 1924, Amy and Edwin Earhart's troubled, 29-year marriage finally ended in divorce. The three Earhart women now decided to return to the East Coast. Muriel, who had signed up for a series of education courses at Harvard, went on ahead; Amelia announced that she and her mother would fly east in the Kinner Canary. The rest of the family, however, was decidedly unenthusiastic about the cross-country flight plan.

Because of their objections and because her sinus problem had flared up again, Earhart reluctantly agreed to sell her plane and buy a car for the trip. She replaced the Canary with a vehicle she named "The Yellow Peril"—a bright yellow touring car complete with running boards and sporty wire wheels.

Amy, Amelia, and Muriel Earhart moved into a comfortable house in Medford, a quiet Boston suburb. As soon as they were settled, Earhart entered the hospital, hoping to obtain surgical relief from the severe sinus headaches and nasal pain that continued to plague her. At Massachusetts General Hospital doctors removed a small piece of bone from her nose to allow for natural drainage. For the first time in years she was free of pain.

Earhart spent the next year restlessly, making up and then changing her mind about what occupation to pursue. She reenrolled as a premedical student at Columbia, dropped out again, got a job teaching English to foreign students in Boston, took summer courses at Harvard. She was now 28 years old, unmarried, and uncertain of her future.

In the fall of 1926, she answered an advertisement in a local paper for a part-time job at Denison House, a Boston community center serving a "melting pot" neighborhood. Most of the area's residents were poor Syrian, Chinese, Greek, and Russian Jewish immigrants.

Despite Earhart's lack of experience in social work, Denison House manager Marion Perkins hired her at once. "She always seemed to me," Perkins later recalled, "an unusual mixture of the artist and the practical person."

Earhart's principal duty at Denison House was teaching English to foreign-born children and adults. She had grown up among middle-class midwesterners and had gone to school with the pampered daughters of the rich. This area of Boston seemed exotic; here she discovered, as she later wrote, "manners and modes very different from those with which I was familiar"; they fascinated her.

Earhart threw herself into her new world. She made friends with local people, happily accepting their invitations to join them at family meals. Many women of Earhart's background regarded working with the poor as a form of charity, but she had a different viewpoint. "Social work," she wrote later, "does not begin and end with philanthropy." She believed that helping others meant educating them, showing them how to build a springboard from which to escape poverty and illiteracy.

Earhart shared this house in Medford, Massachusetts, with her mother and sister during the mid-1920s, but she spent most of her time at the community center where she was employed as a social worker.

Earhart was deeply immersed in her job. Her year-end notes to herself reflected her preoccupation with it: "I shall try to keep contact with the women who have come to class; Mrs. S. and her drunken husband, Mrs. F.'s struggle to get her husband here, Mrs. Z. to get her papers in the face of all odds. . . ."

After a year at Denison House, Earhart was made a full-time staff member. Put in charge of girls between the ages of 5 and 14, she was assigned an apartment at the community center and given a raise to $60 per month. She was a great favorite with the children, especially when they found out she had actually flown an airplane. She delighted them with rides in "The Yellow Peril," often taking them to her house in Medford for backyard picnics and storytelling sessions around the fire.

Sam Chapman had followed Earhart east and gotten a job as an engineer with a Boston electric company. He and Earhart frequently joined her sister and her fiancé, Albert Morrissey, for weekend swims and cookouts along the shore. Although she spent a good deal of time with Chapman, Earhart's insistence on living at Denison House was a bone of contention; he thought the immigrant children were taking up too much of her time and affection.

Chapman wanted to marry Earhart, but he rejected the idea of a working wife. Nevertheless, he proposed to her. Unwilling to give up her freedom for what she called "the life of a domestic robot," she quickly turned him down.

Chapman thought Earhart had rejected his proposal because she resented the irregular hours required by his job, and he volunteered to make adjustments. "I'll be whatever you want me to be," she remembered him saying. "I'll get other work tomorrow if you say so."

Far from being swayed by Chapman's conciliatory approach, Earhart was put off by his willingness to give up his own career. "I don't want to tell Sam what to do," she told her sister. "He ought to know what makes him happiest, and then do it, no matter what other people say. I know what I want to do and I expect to do it, married or single!" The courtship was over, but Earhart and Chapman remained friends for the rest of her life.

It was while she and Chapman were having their dialogue about marriage that Earhart wrote the poem "Courage":

> Courage is the price that Life exacts for
>   granting peace.
> The soul that knows it not
> Knows no release from little things,
> Knows not the livid loneliness of fear,
> Nor mountain heights where bitter joy
>   can hear
> The sound of wings.
>
> How can life grant us boon of living,
>   compensate
> For dull gray ugliness and pregnant hate
> Unless we dare
> The soul's dominion? Each time we
>   make a choice, we pay
> With courage to behold the resistless
>   day,
> And count it fair.

In an effort to forget her broken romance, Earhart redoubled her dedication to her friends at Denison House. When,

Sam Chapman asked Earhart to marry him, but he wanted a homemaker, not a pilot, as a wife. Earhart was fond of him, but she turned him down. She had no wish, she said, to become a "domestic robot."

for example, a Syrian boy was blinded by the explosion of a kerosene heater, it was she who drove him three times a week to a school where he took lessons in Braille, a special system of reading and writing for the blind.

Ruth Nichols (right) meets fellow aviator Amelia Earhart at a 1928 Boston party. The two women were to be frequent rivals for aviation records but their friendship, based on their mutual love of flying, proved enduring.

Commenting on her assistant's attitude, Marion Perkins later wrote, "Youth, keeping a heart, soul, and body that are wide open to all the rich opportunities of life—that is part of Amelia's creed."

Although Earhart found deep satisfaction in her work at Denison House, she could never quite forget the exhilaration, the exalted loneliness of her solo flights over Los Angeles. She had never felt so vibrantly alive, so free from petty cares, as when she was winging high over the mountain tops or soaring out across the sea. She began flying again on the weekends, mainly as an agent for aircraft manufacturer W. G. Kinner, demonstrating planes for potential buyers.

After joining the Boston chapter of the National Aeronautic Association, Earhart decided to try to organize a new fliers' group. In September 1927 she wrote to fellow aviator Ruth Nichols: "What do you think of the advisability of forming an organization composed of women who fly? Personally, I am a social worker who flies for sport. I cannot claim to be a feminist but do rather enjoy seeing women tackling all kinds of new problems—new for them, that is."

What was to be a long and close friendship between Earhart and Nichols was launched, but organizational plans would have to wait. In April 1928, while rehearsing a play with the young people at Denison House, Earhart received a telephone call that would change her life forever. Nothing, neither work nor play, would ever be quite the same again.

Every inch a pilot, Earhart wears leather from head to toe in this pensive photograph, one of her mother's favorites.

SIX

"An American Girl of the Right Image"

The voice on the telephone was deep and masculine. "My name is Railey," it said. "Captain Hilton Railey."

"Yes?" said Earhart.

"You're interested in flying, I understand?"

"I certainly am."

"Miss Earhart, would you be willing to do something important for the cause of aviation?"

"Such as what?" Her tone was skeptical.

"Flying a plane across the Atlantic Ocean."

Was the call a hoax? Earhart demanded references. Railey told her he ran a public relations firm whose clients included such aviation notables as Ruth Nichols and Commander Richard E. Byrd, the celebrated polar explorer.

Later that day, with Marion Perkins along as a witness, Earhart met Railey at a Boston hotel. There he told her that a wealthy, American-born British woman named Amy Guest had purchased Byrd's plane, a trimotor Fokker. Guest wanted the plane, which she had renamed the *Friendship*, flown across the Atlantic as a good-will gesture between the United States and Great Britain. She had hired two expert male pilots to make the flight, but she insisted that "an American girl of the right image" go along too. How, asked Railey, would Earhart like to be that "American girl"—the first woman ever to fly the Atlantic Ocean?

Earhart hesitated for only a second. Then she said yes.

"Only a flicker in her cool eyes betrayed the excitement the question must have aroused," Railey would recall.

Ten days later Earhart was in New York City, being interviewed by publisher George Palmer Putnam, attorney David T. Layman, and John Phipps, all associates of Railey. They barraged her with questions. How many hours did she have in the air? What was her education? How strong was she? What would she do after the flight?

In her book *The Fun of It*, Earhart gave an amused account of the interview. "If I were found wanting on too many counts I should be deprived of a trip," she wrote. "On the other hand, if I were just too fascinating the gallant gentlemen might be loath to drown me. It was therefore necessary for me to maintain an attitude of impenetrable mediocrity."

Earhart needed only a few words to express her real reaction to the proposition: "When a great adventure's offered," she said, "you don't refuse it."

Poised, intelligent, confident, now with many hours of solo experience behind her, Amelia Earhart was the ideal choice for the flight. And for publisher George Putnam, the flight looked like the perfect

As Richard Byrd looks on, Earhart meets Amy Guest, sponsor of the 1928 Friendship flight. Guest had wanted to make the trip herself, but was persuaded to select an "American girl of the right image" instead.

chance to create a best-selling book. Putnam had already published two extremely successful aviation books: *Skyward* by Commander Byrd, and *We* by Charles Lindbergh, the daring pilot who, in 1927, had been the first to fly alone across the Atlantic. There was sure to be a book on Amelia Earhart. She even looked like Charles Lindbergh, with the same slim frame, the same serious gray eyes, the same short, fair hair. The project was a publicity man's dream.

Earhart returned to Boston and arranged for a leave of absence from Denison House. Because the flight's backers wanted to avoid advance publicity, which might inspire competitors to plan a transatlantic race, all preparations were kept secret. Earhart told Sam Chapman what to do with her possessions if she did not return, but she did not reveal her plans to her family. To them, she wrote what she cheerfully called "popping off letters." The letters were to be delivered only if the plane crashed.

To her sister she wrote, "If I succeed, all will be well. If I don't, I shall be happy to pop off in the midst of such an adventure." Part of the letter to her mother said, "Even though I have lost the adventure it was worthwhile. Our family tends to be too secure. My life has really been very happy and I didn't mind contemplating its end in the midst of it." To her father she said, "Hooray for the last great adventure!"

Although she was cautioned to stay away from the airfield where the plane was being readied for flight, Earhart could not resist one look at the plane. "When I first saw *Friendship*, she was jacked up

Mechanics work on the Friendship *at a Boston airfield. The trimotor Fokker was designed as a land plane, but when Amy Guest decided to have it flown over the ocean, its wheels were exchanged for pontoons.*

in the shadows of a hangar in East Boston," she wrote later. "The ship's golden wings with their spread of 72 feet were strong and exquisitely fashioned." Originally a land plane, the Fokker was fitted with pontoons in anticipation of a forced ocean landing. The cabin was crowded with two large gas tanks and a navigation table. All passenger seats had been removed.

While she was waiting for work on the *Friendship* to be completed, Earhart often met with Wilmer Stultz and Louis "Slim" Gordon, the pilots with whom she would cross the ocean. Their conferences were held at the Boston residence of Commander Byrd, the project's technical adviser.

By mid-May 1928 the *Friendship* was ready to fly, but takeoff was delayed by a persistent fog that enveloped Boston. At dawn on June 3, the weather cleared at last, and the plane roared into the sky, heading for Trepassey, Newfoundland. There it would be refueled for the flight across the Atlantic.

At the controls was "Bill" Stultz; Gordon sat next to him and Earhart crouched in a small space behind the fuel tanks. She wore a helmet and goggles, a brown leather jacket, breeches, and boots. "There seems to be a feeling that a woman preparing to drop in on England, so to speak, ought to have something of a wardrobe," she commented later, but on this journey her "single elegance," as she put it, was a brightly printed silk scarf. With cabin space at a premium, the *Friendship*'s crew brought almost no luggage. "Toilet articles began with a toothbrush and ended with a comb," noted Earhart.

The plane was barely off the ground when George Putnam called a news conference. The news crackled around the world: An American woman had just left Boston by air; destination, England! Reporters converged on the Earhart house in Medford, demanding information about the woman flier and, ironically, giving Amy Earhart her first knowledge of her daughter's flight.

Earhart, meanwhile, was heading north and making notes in the *Friendship*'s logbook:

"7 o'clock. Slim has the controls and Bill is tuning in. I squat on the floor."

"There is a small steamer to the right. I wonder if he knows who we are. I wonder if we know...."

"The sea looks like the back of an elephant, the same kind of wrinkles...."

"The motors are humming sweetly."

Forced by bad weather to spend the night at Halifax, Nova Scotia, the *Friendship* arrived in Trepassey on June 4. It was greeted by a swarm of small boats, their decks crowded with cheering fishermen. Earhart sent her mother a wire, urging her not to worry. Amy Earhart wired back with characteristic enthusiasm: "We are not worrying. Wish I were with you. Good luck and cheerio. Love, Mother."

At Trepassey, bad weather locked the crew in for two weeks. Each attempt to get the *Friendship* into the air was thwarted by heavy rain and fog. The days became a blur of false starts and nonstop gin rummy games. Stultz was a highly skilled pilot and a first-class navigator, but he had a major problem. Like Earhart's father, he was an alcoholic. The combination of tension and boredom during the long days at Trepassey triggered a drinking binge that unnerved both Earhart and Gordon.

In her book *The Fun of It* Earhart wrote lightly of the days at Trepassey, but they were hard on her. Gordon wanted to send for a backup pilot from Boston, but Earhart had no desire to humiliate Stultz. Furthermore, she had had experience in dealing with drinkers, and she believed she could sober him up when it was time to take off.

On June 17 "Doc" Kimball of the U.S. Weather Bureau in New York reported fair weather over the North Atlantic for the next two days. The news found Stultz in an alcoholic haze. Earhart and Gordon almost literally dragged him into the *Friendship*'s cockpit. There, to his colleagues' immense relief, he seemed suddenly sober.

Stultz taxied across the choppy waters of Trepassey's harbor, trying to get up enough speed for takeoff. On his fourth effort, as the speed gauge passed 50 miles an hour, the *Friendship* was airborne.

For the next 20 hours and 40 minutes Earhart knelt at the chart table, filling the

Waiting for news about her daughter's 1928 transatlantic flight, Amy Earhart tunes the radio at her home in Medford. She knew nothing of the journey until reporters gathered at her door after the takeoff.

log with notes on the weather, airspeeds, altitudes, and compass markings. She frequently alternated technical data with personal comments, describing clouds as "marvelous shapes in white ... trailing shimmering veils," and wondering if the plane could "bounce forever on the packed fog."

Between log entries and brief naps she gazed from the plane's window. "I think I am happy," she wrote. "I am getting housemaid's knee kneeling here at the table gulping beauty."

Flying at 11,000 feet at one point, the plane encountered a bank of clouds "piled like fantastic gobs of mashed potatoes." Stultz, who did not want to spend precious fuel in an attempt to climb above the cloudbank, nosed the plane down. The descent was not easy. "Going down fast," wrote Earhart. "It takes a lot to make my ears hurt. 5,000 now. Awfully wet. Water dripping in window."

The last hour of the trip was by far the worst. The aviators were beset by storms and heavy fog. By the time the sun came

After learning that the strange aircraft in their harbor has flown across the Atlantic Ocean, residents of Burry Port, Wales, gather along the shore for a glimpse of the daring American crew.

Earhart stands on one of the Friendship's pontoons as she waits for a lift to shore at Burry Port.

up, the weather was calmer but the radio was dead. The plane had one hour's supply of fuel left, the crew was exhausted, and the pilot was unsure about his position. At 8:30 A.M. Earhart's logbook entry read, "Try to get bearing. Radio won't. One hr's gas. Mess."

When Stultz sighted an ocean liner below, Earhart hastily scribbled a note, asking the ship's crew to paint its position in big letters on its deck. As Stultz circled frantically, she put the message in a bag, weighted it with an orange, and dropped it through the hatch. The package missed, plunging unnoticed into the sea. The steamer continued on its course and the *Friendship* pressed on through the fog.

Spirits in the cockpit had reached their lowest point when the aviators spotted fishing boats below and, looming through the mist, a solid blue shadow.

Land!

After skirting the cliffs, looking down on what Earhart later described as a "storybook countryside of neatly kept hedges, compact fields, and roadways lined with trees," Stultz brought the plane down in a small harbor. They had landed at Burry Port, Wales.

The arrival of the *Friendship* added three names to the short list of men who had crossed the Atlantic by air. And one of those names belonged to a woman.

The weary crew tied the plane to a buoy and waited for a boat to come out and pick them up. Burry Port, however, was not expecting them; the *Friendship*, for all they knew, might have come from 10 miles away. Men working near the harbor gave the plane little more than a curious glance.

"They looked us over," wrote Earhart later, "waded down to shore, and then calmly turned their backs and went to work again." The crew was finally brought ashore; Hilton Railey, who had flown over from London, was there to greet them.

"Congratulations!" he shouted at Earhart. "How does it feel to be the first woman to have flown the Atlantic?"

"Like a sack of potatoes," she said, smiling and shrugging her shoulders. "Bill did all the flying. I was just baggage."

Despite her repeated refusal to take any credit for the success of the flight, Earhart was an instant celebrity. In 1928 the mere fact that she was a woman and had arrived in Great Britain by way of the sky made her a hero. "From the beginning," she regretfully observed, "it was evident the accident of sex made me the chief performer in our particular sideshow."

Wilmer Stultz, Amelia Earhart, and "Slim" Gordon wave to New Yorkers during a parade welcoming them home after their 1928 flight to Wales.

SEVEN

America's Flying Sweetheart

News of the *Friendship*'s transatlantic flight traveled fast. After the three weary fliers had caught up with their sleep in a Welsh hotel, they refueled their plane and, with Earhart at the controls, flew to Southampton, England. Here and in London, their next stop, they found themselves the center of wildly enthusiastic crowds of well-wishers, autograph seekers, reporters, newsreel cameramen, and speechmaking civic officials.

Earhart was genuinely distressed by the special attention focused on her. "All I did," she insisted, "was lie on my tummy and take pictures of clouds." She tried hard, as she wrote later, "to make them realize that all the credit belonged to the boys," but her efforts were useless.

A picture caption in one of the first stories about Earhart said, "She Has the Lindbergh Look." Charles Lindbergh had been one of the world's best known and best loved celebrities since 1927, when he had made the first solo flight across the Atlantic. Now the public had a female counterpart for "The Lone Eagle"; Earhart quickly became known as "Lady Lindy."

The 30-year-old Earhart was embar-

rassed by the comparison. Lindbergh had been a courageous and independent pioneer; she had been, she kept saying, only a "sack of potatoes" on the flight of the *Friendship*. Nevertheless, the nickname stuck; the world, it seemed, could not lavish enough praise and affection on "Lady Lindy."

When the three aviators arrived in London, a congratulatory cable awaited; it was from U.S. President Calvin Coolidge, and it was addressed to Amelia Earhart. She quickly wired her response: "Success entirely due great skill of Mr. Stultz. He was only one mile off-course ... after flying blind for 2,246 miles."

The next two weeks, noted Earhart later, were "a jumble of teas, theaters, speechmaking, exhibition tennis, polo, and Parliament, with hundreds of faces crowded in." She was sought out by such leading Britons as Lady Astor, the Prince of Wales (later King Edward VIII), and future British prime minister Winston Churchill. Swamped with telegrams, letters, invitations, and requests for interviews, she did her patient best to answer them all.

Wrote Hilton Railey, "She remained

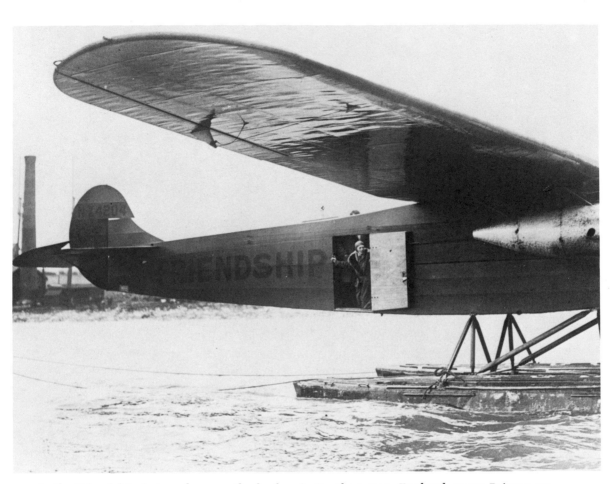

As the Friendship *is towed across the harbor in Southampton, England, eager Britons get their first view of "Lady Lindy."*

herself, serious, forthright, with no bunk in her makeup. Even in those days I sensed that she would yet write drama in the skies. Her simplicity would capture people everywhere; her strength of character would hold her on her course; in calm pursuit of an end not personal she would achieve greatness. To me, in fact, she seemed that she had been born with it."

Earhart was sure the fanfare would stop soon; when it did, she would once again be simply a social worker who flew

"for the fun of it." Accompanied by Railey, Stultz, and Gordon, she sailed for the United States aboard the ocean liner *President Roosevelt* on June 28. Before she left, she bought a small plane, an Avro Avian Moth, from Lady Mary Heath, one of England's foremost women pilots. She arranged to have the plane—in which Heath had made the first solo flight from South Africa to Egypt—shipped home.

Even on shipboard, Earhart was besieged by admirers. The *Roosevelt*'s captain was sympathetic to his famous

A beaming Amy Guest (left) brings the crew of the Friendship *ashore in Southampton. Next to Guest are (left to right) Gordon, Earhart, Stultz, and the mayor of Southampton.*

passenger's need for privacy, and tried to see that she was left alone. He also gave her lessons in celestial navigation (navigation by the stars), an important aviation technique she had not yet mastered.

During the crossing, a news report on the ship's radio revealed that New York City was planning an all-out celebration for the fliers, Earhart in particular. The news distressed her. "I'm a false heroine," she told Railey. "And that makes me feel guilty." It was a feeling that would dog her for years.

When the *Roosevelt* docked in New York, a small army of dignitaries whisked the three aviators off the ship for a triumphal ride through the harbor. At City Hall, they received medals and keys to the city; paraded down Broadway in open cars, they were almost buried in a blizzard of confetti. Letters and invitations to visit poured in from cities all over the country.

Everywhere she went Earhart was straightforward about her part in the venture, repeatedly giving credit to Stultz and Gordon. The legend, however, had already been born; Amelia Earhart, "First Lady of the Sky," had become America's flying sweetheart.

Publisher George Putnam was now playing an increasingly large role in Earhart's life. It was Putnam who planned her lecture schedule, he who advised her which commercial products to endorse and which press interviews to grant. Overwhelmed by her sudden rise to fame, Earhart was grateful for his help.

Putnam, 39 years old, was a graduate of Harvard and the University of California. He had headed an expedition to Greenland, served as mayor of a small midwestern town, and written several adventure books. Impatient and energetic, he had a gift for propelling others to celebrity status and keeping them there.

Eager to publish a book about Earhart's part in the transatlantic flight, Putnam offered her an impressive contract. He even gave her a place to write: the handsome, secluded house he shared with his wife and two young sons in the New York City suburb of Rye. Earhart was soon hard at work on what was to become *20 Hrs. 40 Min.*

When she was not writing, Earhart was conferring with Putnam about product endorsements and lecture offers; educators and promoters all over the country wanted her to speak about her *Friendship* experience to clubs and student groups. *Cosmopolitan* magazine asked her to write a regular column on aviation, and she accepted with delight. Here was a chance to alert young women everywhere to the possibilities awaiting them, not only in aviation but in all kinds of careers.

When she finished her book in Septem-

The Friendship's *flight was a popular subject for satirists in 1928. Here, a diehard male chauvinist reacts to the news that a "gal" has crossed the Atlantic by air.*

ber, Earhart decided to take a break. Finally admitting that a return to Denison House would be a step backward in her life, she bought a set of air navigation maps and headed for California in her new Avian Moth.

In Los Angeles she visited her father, saw old friends, and attended the National Air Races. When she flew back to New York, she had created a new aviation record: she was the first woman to make a round-trip solo flight between the nation's East and West Coasts.

"Goggles cannot be abandoned on long hops," she wrote later of the cross-country trip. "They, of course, bequeath sunburned rings of white around the eye. In my logbook I noted that when and if I reached Los Angeles, I should resemble a horned toad."

Earhart now had money in her pocket, an office at *Cosmopolitan*, a book on the stands, and a capable, dedicated manager to handle incoming offers. But for the moment, she said, all she "wished to do in the world was to be a vagabond—in the air."

During her lazy days of "vagabonding," Earhart was dreaming of the future, of setting new records, of making new flights. But flying cost money. What better way to make it, she thought, than to lecture to all the people clamoring to hear her? If 20 lectures would pay for a long "hop," then 20 lectures she would give.

20 Hrs. 40 Min. was a great success, increasing the demands for personal appearances by Earhart. Putnam soon arranged her first lecture schedule, and for the next year she tirelessly toured the country, often speaking in as many as 27 cities in one month. She addressed colleges, women's clubs, civic and professional organizations, impressing audiences with her candid and modest views.

On trains or in hotel rooms between speaking engagements, Earhart wrote articles for *Cosmopolitan*. She suddenly became every girl's glamorous big sister, every woman's sympathetic daughter. In such articles as "Try Flying Yourself!" "Is It Safe to Fly?" and "Why Are Women Afraid to Fly?" she demystified the new world of aviation, urging women to explore it for themselves. Hundreds of letters poured in daily from women seeking advice on everything from careers to marriage.

After the Friendship *flight, Earhart was often compared to Charles Lindbergh. The parallel distressed her; she considered his role heroic and her own no more important than "a sack of potatoes."*

Through Putnam's efforts, photographs of "Lady Lindy" appeared in newspapers across the country. The warm smile, the cropped hair, the clear, calm gaze, the well-tailored slacks, the coolly independent stance, all spoke directly to American women, alerting them to a world of exciting new possibilities. In a matter of months she had come to symbolize the independent spirit of modern womanhood.

In addition to her lecture tours, Earhart began to travel for Transcontinental Air Transport, a new airline whose managerial staff included Charles Lindbergh. It was Earhart's job to stimulate passenger interest, especially among women.

About to begin a 1931 cross-country "hop" to promote Beech-Nut products, Earhart boards an autogiro in Newark, New Jersey. The trip was one of many commercial ventures organized by Earhart's husband, George Putnam.

When Lindbergh and his wife Anne met Earhart, they warmed to her immediately. In her book *Hour of Gold, Hour of Lead* Anne Lindbergh wrote, "She is the most amazing person—just as tremendous as Charles, I think. It startles me how much they are alike in breadth. She has the clarity of mind, impersonal eye, coolness of temperament, balance of a scientist."

In spite of all her hours in the air and her dazzling reputation as a flier, Earhart still felt deficient in some important flying skills. She could handle a plane with easy confidence, but she knew little about navigation, "blind flying," or using a two-way radio.

Earhart was troubled by the thought that her reputation was based more on publicity than on actual accomplishment. Determined to prove worthy of the public's faith in her, she sold her Avian Moth in the summer of 1929 and bought a secondhand Lockheed Vega. She flew the more powerful, high-wing monoplane to Santa Monica, California; there she entered the Women's Air Derby, the first cross-country competition solely for women.

The event had been dubbed "The Powder Puff Derby" by amused male observers. To the race's 20 women competitors, however, it was no joke. All of them were eager to prove that women had a rightful place in the future of American aviation, to demonstrate that members of their sex deserved more appropriate nicknames than "ladybirds" and "flying flappers." Furthermore, the winner of the race would receive $2,500, a substantial sum in 1929.

Earhart's hairstyle was copied by thousands of American women. One newspaper editor, exasperated by the "Earhart look," offered the aviator some free advice. "Comb your head, kid," he said, "comb your head!"

Among the entrants were most of the well-known women fliers of the day. In addition to Earhart, they included long-distance aviator Ruth Nichols; Louise Thaden, holder of the women's speed record; Marvel Crosson, a young but experienced commercial pilot from Alaska; and Gladys O'Donnell, who was highly skilled in closed-circuit racing.

Participants in the race, which began on August 18, were scheduled to fly from

Santa Monica to Cleveland, Ohio, in nine daily segments of approximately 300 miles each. The pilots took off each day in a designated order. Flying over mountains and deserts, they were guided only by compasses and road maps. Fifteen of the twenty entrants arrived in Cleveland; accidents stopped four, and death claimed one.

Marvel Crosson bailed out when her engine malfunctioned over Arizona; her parachute failed to open, and she plummeted to her death. In Columbus, Ohio, almost at the end of the race, a gust of wind blew Ruth Nichols's plane into a tractor parked near the runway. Next in line for takeoff, Earhart dashed to the res-cue. She pulled her friend to safety but lost her turn to take off. Thaden was first in Cleveland; O'Donnell came in second and Earhart third.

Three months after the Women's Derby a group of its participants formed an all-female aviation society. Its charter members were 99 licensed women pilots, its name was the Ninety-Nines. With Earhart as its first president, the Ninety-Nines concentrated on creating new and expanded opportunities for women in aviation. High on the agenda for many of the members was a trip that would, they believed, erase any remaining public doubts about women as pilots: a solo flight across the Atlantic.

Participants in the 1929 Women's Air Derby line up for a group portrait. Among the entrants are Gladys O'Donnell (third from left), Louise Thaden (fifth from right), and (fourth from right) Amelia Earhart.

The most determined of these would-be transatlantic fliers were Amelia Earhart and Ruth Nichols. Nichols was ready in September 1931, but bad weather forced her to postpone her flight until the following spring. While she was waiting, she decided to try for a nonstop distance record, flying from California to New York. After she broke the record—by flying 1,977 miles—a storm forced her down in Louisville, Kentucky. During a takeoff the next day, her plane caught fire. Nichols escaped with her life but the plane exploded, ending her chance to be the first woman to fly solo across the Atlantic.

Earhart still felt she needed more training before she entered the Atlantic-solo sweepstakes. Answering a friend who urged her to plan a trip soon after the Air Derby, she said, "It would be foolish for me to attempt it until I've had considerably more flying and navigation experience. Give me, say, 18 months to two years and then we'll see." She began taking navigational instruction from weather expert "Doc" Kimball. The Earhart-Kimball alliance would be an important one. On the long "hops" that were to be the crowning achievements of her career, Earhart never left the ground without weather clearance from Kimball.

Earhart visited each of her divorced parents as often as she could and, as her income increased, began to assume responsibility for their debts. She paid off the mortgage on her father's new house in California and often sent her mother gifts of money and clothing. Edwin Earhart's health had been declining sharply; in the fall of 1930 his illness was diagnosed as inoperable stomach cancer. His

Edwin Earhart stayed in close touch with his famous daughter after his alcoholism had alienated his wife and many of his friends. His death in 1930 was a heavy blow to the aviator.

daughter flew from New York to the West Coast to see him, arriving a week before his death.

Earhart wrote home to her mother, "He asked about you and Pidge [Muriel's nickname] a lot, and I faked telegrams for him from you all. He was an aristocrat as he went—all the weaknesses gone, with a little boy's brown puzzled eyes." Despite her father's drinking problem, Amelia Earhart had retained her devotion to him, and his death hit her hard. She was busy with her lectures, her work for Transcontinental Air, her endless fan mail, her flying, her courses of instruction. She was, however, lonely.

George Putnam and his wife had been divorced late in 1929; five times after that, Putnam had asked Earhart to marry him. Five times, she had said no. "I'm still unsold on marriage," she wrote to a friend. "I don't want anything all of the time. I think I may not be able to see marriage except as a cage until I am unfit to work or fly or be active and of course I would not be desirable then."

Soon after her father's death, Earhart received her sixth marriage proposal from Putnam. This time she surprised him—as well as her family, friends, and much of the public—and said yes. Amy Earhart objected to Putnam, who was 10

Earhart and George Putnam share a quiet moment at home after their 1931 wedding. The aviator, who regarded marriage as "an attractive cage" at best, had accepted Putnam only after his sixth proposal.

years older than her daughter, but Earhart had made up her mind. Unlike Sam Chapman, who had been unwilling to share her with her work, Putnam respected and encouraged her independence. He believed, as Earhart said, in "wives doing what they do best."

Earhart married Putnam in a quiet ceremony at his mother's Connecticut home on February 7, 1931. Before they exchanged vows, she handed him a most unusual marriage contract. Putnam later described it as "brutal in its frankness but beautiful in its honesty."

"Dear GP," the letter said, "there are some things which should be writ before we are married. Things we have talked over before—most of them.

"You must know again my reluctance to marry, my feeling that I shatter thereby chances in work which means so much to me. I feel the move just now as foolish as anything I could do. I know there may be compensations, but have no heart to look ahead.

"In our life together I shall not hold you to any medieval code of faithfulness to me, nor shall I consider myself bound to you similarly. If we can be honest I think the differences which arise may best be avoided.

"Please let us not interfere with each other's work or play, nor let the world see private joys or disagreements. In this connection I may have to keep some place where I can go to be myself now and then, for I cannot guarantee to endure at all times the confinements of even an attractive cage.

"I must exact a cruel promise, and this is that you will let me go in a year if we

Many Americans were shocked to see Earhart's face in this 1928 cigarette advertisement. Regretting her endorsement, she donated her $1,500 payment to Richard Byrd's upcoming Antarctic expedition.

find no happiness together. I will try to do my best in every way."

After the wedding, Putnam promoted Earhart's career with renewed vigor. He encouraged her to begin a second book, *The Fun of It*, organized innumerable promotional tours, and arranged for her sponsorship of a variety of products. These included successful lines of Amelia Earhart luggage, women's clothing, and stationery.

Advertising everything from automobiles to pajamas, her picture appeared in newspapers and magazines and on billboards across the country. Putnam even allowed Earhart's name and photograph

to be used in cigarette advertisements, despite the fact that she was a non-smoker. Promoting Beech-Nut foods, she spent 150 hours flying an autogiro lettered with the company's name. The proceeds from the lecture tours, books, and commercial endorsements all went into the kitty to finance future flights.

Earhart was pleasantly surprised by marriage; "I am much happier," she wrote her mother, "than I expected I could ever be in that state." She trusted her husband's judgment, although she occasionally felt he went too far in his eagerness to commercialize her name. When Putnam approved a shoddy line of children's hats bearing her signature, she objected strenuously. "This," he recalled her saying, "won't do at all." He pointed out that the manufacturer had a contract and had already made the hats. "Then he can unmake them!" said Earhart. "I won't be a party to cheating kids."

Addressing women's groups across America, Earhart talked about marriage. "The effect of having other interests beyond those exclusively domestic works well," she said in one speech. "The more one does and feels, the more one is able to do. . . . Women seem to regard marriage as a highly honorable retreat from business failure. They think they are after freedom but what I'm afraid they want is lack of responsibility. . . . Marriage is a mutual responsibility and I cannot see why husbands shouldn't share in the responsibility of the home."

Earhart was by now a dedicated feminist with a firm belief in equal rights and equal opportunities for all. She often spoke out for the repeal of laws that dis-

Newsreel cameramen and reporters zero in on the open car carrying the Friendship *crew away from Chicago's Union Station in 1928. The fliers were met by cheering crowds in every city they visited.*

criminated against women. "Sex," she said, "has been used much too long as a subterfuge. It has become pretty evident that the female of the species is not so radically different from the male. . . . I am not one to set any boundaries upon the work of men or women nor restrict them except by the natural laws of individual aptitude."

A committed pacifist as well as a feminist, Earhart insisted that if war was to be tolerated, women should be drafted along with men. In one speech she said, "Drafting women for the real work of war—not the pretty sideline jobs where you can wear giddy uniforms and not get dirtied up—would make war much less inviting to males. . . . If [men] had women with them, greasy, dirty women with guns in their hands, the glamour and glory of killing would soon fade. I suspect that men might rather vacate the arena altogether than share it with women."

Addressing a meeting of the ultraconservative Daughters of the American Revolution in Washington, D.C., Earhart deliberately raised hackles. "You know," she said, "you really shouldn't have invited me here. I always say what I think and you may not like it." Talking about war, she told the women, "You glorify it. You applaud the marching feet and the band and you cheer on the military machine. You really all ought to be drafted." Not surprisingly, the applause following that particular speech was restrained.

No matter how many speeches she made, how many cross-country flights she made, how many records she set, Earhart still felt there was something fraudulent about her fame. She did not believe she had fairly earned the title of premier female flier of the world. One morning at breakfast she lowered her newspaper and fixed her husband with a thoughtful stare. "Would you mind if I flew the Atlantic?" she asked. George Putnam's reply was unnecessary. He knew from the look on her face that she had already made her decision.

U.S. newspapers ran this shot of "Miss Amelia Earhart, attractive woman aviator and the first of her sex to fly the Atlantic," when she wed "wealthy and prominent publisher" George Putnam in 1931.

After her transatlantic solo, Earhart displayed almost superhuman patience, agreeably posing with her beloved Vega for the countless pictures demanded by news photographers.

EIGHT

From the Atlantic to the Pacific

On May 21, 1932, when Earhart climbed stiffly out of the cockpit of her plane in Londonderry, Ireland, she was exhausted but exuberant. Her dream had come true; she had crossed the vast Atlantic alone, the first woman in history to do so.

A whirlwind of banquets, parades, press interviews, and awards followed her arrival in Europe, but no gold medal shone brighter than the glowing sense of accomplishment Earhart felt within herself. "To want in one's own heart to do a thing for its own sake," she wrote, "to concentrate all one's energies upon it—that is not only the surest guarantee of its success, it is also being true to oneself."

As George Putnam headed for England aboard an ocean liner, his wife was listening to cheering crowds and an unending stream of congratulatory speeches. She was made an honorary member of the British Guild of Airpilots and Navigators, and toasted by the British Institute of Journalists. Especially touched by a standing ovation from British reporters, she said, "The nicest thing that has happened to me is having all these men stand and sing 'For she's a jolly good fellow!'"

Earhart and Putnam went from London to Paris, where she received another tumultuous welcome. She was presented with the Cross of the Legion of Honor and mobbed by excited Parisians whenever she appeared in public. The couple went on to Rome, where they met with government leaders and Pope Pius XI, and to Belgium, where they dined with King Christian X.

On June 15 Earhart and Putnam sailed for the United States on the *Ile de France*. The liner was escorted to sea by airplanes that dropped flowers and dipped their wings in salute to "Lady Lindy." A week later the couple was in Constitution Hall in Washington, D.C.

As the U.S. Marine band played "Hail to the Chief," Earhart, radiant in a long white gown, entered on the arm of President Herbert Hoover. Present were Supreme Court Chief Justice Charles Evans Hughes, and most of the nation's senators, congressmen, high-ranking military officers, and important scientists, as well

Italian officials welcome Earhart to Rome with roses and smiles. Throngs of Romans mobbed the aviator when she appeared on the streets, sometimes snatching at her clothing in hopes of getting a souvenir.

as dozens of foreign dignitaries. After Earhart had received the National Geographic Society's coveted Special Gold Medal for distinction in aviation, Hoover addressed the audience.

Earhart's accomplishments, said the president, had "not been won by the selfish pursuit of a purely personal ambition, but as part of a career generously animated by a wish to help others share in the rich opportunities of life, and by a wish also to enlarge those opportunities by expanding the powers of women."

Earhart's response was typically self-effacing. "I think," she said, "that the appreciation of the deed is out of proportion to the deed itself. I shall be happy if my small exploit has drawn attention to the fact that women, too, are flying ." The next day, the Senate and House of Representatives held a special session in which Amelia Earhart was named as the

first woman to receive the Distinguished Flying Cross.

Three months later Earhart set a new women's long-distance record when she flew nonstop from Los Angeles to Newark, New Jersey, in 19 hours and 5 minutes. Eleven months after that, she would break her own record, making the trip in 17 hours 7 1/2 minutes. Honors continued to pour in. "Welcome, thrice welcome, Grand Lady of the Air, crowned glory of earth's womanhood!" read a telegram from the mayor of a city Earhart was due to visit. Amused, Earhart handed the cable to her secretary. "Show this to G.P.," she said, "so he may appreciate me!"

In 1932 Earhart published *The Fun of It*, a warm and spirited account of her various flights to date. The book contained information about the growing field of aviation, snippets of enthusiastic feminism, and short biographies of other women fliers. Like *20 Hrs. 40 Min.*, it was a huge success.

After Franklin and Eleanor Roosevelt moved into the White House in 1933, they frequently entertained Putnam and Earhart, who had become a close friend of the first lady. At a formal dinner party one night, Earhart discovered that Eleanor Roosevelt had never been up for a "hop." She quickly called Eastern Airlines and borrowed a plane. Soon the First Lady of the Land and the First Lady of the Air, both wearing long evening gowns and white gloves, were flying high over Washington.

"AE felt that one's first flight after dark is an experience curiously lovely and significant," recalled Putnam later. After the night flight the two women jumped into

Eleanor Roosevelt's car and took a spin through the dark streets of the capital as Secret Service men looked on in bewilderment.

At the age of 37, Earhart was unquestionably at the top of her profession. Slender and attractive, she was the world's best-known woman pilot, the author of two best-selling books, and the idol of millions of Americans. Still, she was restless. Only new goals and new achievements could satisfy her explorer's soul. Before the excitement about her Atlantic flight had even died down, she began casting about for a new adventure. She wanted to do something no one had ever done before, something bold and dangerous that would tax all her strength.

In 1934 the 2,400 miles between Hawaii

Earhart (left) shares a joke with Eleanor Roosevelt in 1935. The aviator was a frequent guest in the Roosevelt White House.

In a ceremony outside the White House, President Herbert Hoover presents Earhart with a gold medal from the National Geographic Society. He called the pilot one of history's "great pioneering women."

and California were still "virgin" sky. No one, man or woman, had attempted to fly it. It was a complicated route, one that required 14 changes in compass course, all less than one hour apart. But whatever the challenges, Amelia Earhart knew she could meet them. As soon as time and money allowed, she would fly the Pacific Ocean, alone.

With the transpacific flight in mind, Earhart and Putnam moved to California. Earhart had sold her old Lockheed Vega and bought a new one, which was equipped with navigational equipment. Her associate Bernt Balchen was not available to help her prepare for her new journey, but the Putnams' friend Paul Mantz was. Mantz, a highly skilled stunt pilot who had worked in a number of Hollywood films, lived near the Putnams' rented house in North Hollywood. An expert navigator and engineer as well as a superb flier, he was ideally suited for the role of Earhart's technical consultant.

Earhart and Putnam spent much of their leisure time with Mantz and his wife. The two couples played golf, swam, and entertained together. Among their guests were movie stars Mary Pickford and Douglas Fairbanks, cowboy comedian Will Rogers, aviator-explorer Wiley Post, and financier Floyd Odlum, husband of another celebrated flyer, Jacqueline Cochran. California, complete with sunshine, sports, and good friends, delighted Earhart. She liked it even better when her mother, after much persuasion, agreed to leave Massachusetts for a long visit with her daughter.

The Putnams and the Mantzes sailed for Hawaii aboard the S. S. *Lurline* in late

Festooned with leis, Earhart arrives in Honolulu in January 1935. A few days later she became the first person to fly alone from Hawaii to California.

December 1934. Covered by a tarpaulin, Earhart's new Vega was securely tied down to the ship's deck. Although no information about Earhart's plans had been released to the press, the presence of both the famed aviator and her bright red airplane naturally led to suspicions that an important flight was in the offing.

When the *Lurline* docked in Honolulu, Hawaii, Earhart was met with a surprising wave of criticism. It had two causes. First, her prospective flight would take place only a month after another American pilot, Charles Ulm, had been lost while attempting to fly from California to Hawaii. The fruitless, 27-day air and sea search for Ulm had convinced many observers that such a flight was both pointless and dangerous.

Rumors of political manipulation raised even more negative reaction. Hoping to encourage Hawaiian tourism, a group of businessmen had offered a $10,000 prize to the first person to fly from Hawaii to California. Earhart had already planned her flight, but flying was expensive, and news of the prize had been welcome. Now, the group sponsoring Earhart's flight was accused by business rivals of using the well-known aviator as a political pawn. They charged that her prestige would be employed to strengthen the efforts of Hawaiian sugar interests, which were lobbying in Congress for a reduction of taxes on Hawaiian sugar.

Upset by the furor, Earhart's sponsors suggested that she abandon her plans to fly across the Pacific. The aviator was both astonished and furious. She told the sponsors that she detected "an aroma of cowardice" in their suggestion, that any rumors about her political connections were utterly false, and that her plans were unalterable. "I intend to fly to California within this next week," she said icily, "with or without your support." Awed by Earhart's vehemence, the backers meekly agreed to maintain their support.

Four days later Earhart and her Vega were ready to fly, but the weather failed to cooperate. She had planned to take off on the afternoon of January 11, but by 11 o'clock that morning heavy rains had already turned the airfield into a muddy lake, and it was getting worse by the minute.

The Vega, carrying 500 extra gallons of gas as well as radio and navigational aids, weighed more than three tons; getting it off the ground now was going to be difficult, but if Earhart waited much longer, it might be impossible. Weather forecasts indicated that new storms were headed for Hawaii; they might prevent all flights for another 10 days.

At 4:30 in the afternoon the Vega was warmed up and waiting on the runway. Earhart climbed aboard, opened the throttle and released the brakes. As the heavily loaded plane moved slowly down the field, Mantz raced along with it, bellowing, "Get that tail up!" Suddenly, the Vega was airborne.

Earhart passed over Hawaii's Diamond Head at 5,000 feet, climbed, and emerged into a serenely blue evening sky. Then she cranked out her trailing antenna and sent her first radio message. At station KGU in Honolulu, Putnam's voice crackled back, loud and distinct. "It was thrilling to have his voice come in so clear to me, sitting out there over the Pacific. It was really one of the high points of the flight," wrote Earhart later.

From then on it was, she reported, "a night of stars." By midnight the moon had disappeared and a few small rain squalls had begun. She pressed on through the night. At last, she wrote later, "a shadow of light played around the horizon"; soon the sky was filled with blazing sunlight.

In the final hours of the journey Ear-

hart found herself surrounded by a thick blanket of fog. Glancing down through a hole in the fog, she suddenly caught sight of a ship. She dove down through the hole, she wrote later, "faster than I ever flew before from 8,000 feet to 200!" The ship was the *President Pierce*, outward bound from San Francisco. Earhart lined her plane up with the wake of the ship and headed for California—now only 300 miles away!

"There is no doubt that the last hour of any flight is the hardest," she wrote. Confused and weary, the pilot is apt to mistake low cloud formations for land. "I saw considerable territory in the Pacific that California should annex!" she recalled laughingly.

At the Oakland, California, airport, 10,000 people were watching the sky, waiting for Amelia Earhart. Just before noon, a red, high-winged monoplane came in low and fast; without circling the field it landed far down the runway. For a few moments, no one reacted. Then the crowd realized who had just landed, and thousands of cheering people rushed the plane.

Earhart clambered out of the cramped cockpit and grinned broadly. She had been in the air for 18 hours and 15 minutes, and she had set yet another record. "I feel swell," she said.

As news cameras flashed, the crowd screamed and showered her with roses.

Earhart and her Vega appear to float on a sea of humanity at the Oakland airport on January 12, 1935. Her arrival from Hawaii was greeted by 10,000 excited well-wishers.

Radio, along with aviation, had come a long way by 1935. Here, Earhart broadcasts greetings from a radio station in Schenectady, New York, to Commander Richard Byrd in Antarctica. Byrd received her voice loud and clear.

Reporters at the Newark, New Jersey, airport interview Earhart and Putnam after her 1935 Honolulu-to-Oakland flight.

"That landing is something I shall never forget," she said later. "It is in the diary of my heart. It has made Oakland my favorite airport and one of my favorite cities."

By the following March, Earhart was back in New York and ready to begin what she called "the most strenuous lecture engagement ever undertaken." However, when the president of Mexico invited her to visit his country in her trusty Lockheed Vega, she accepted. She immediately plotted a course that would take her from Los Angeles to Mexico City, then across

the Gulf of Mexico to New York, landing in Newark, New Jersey.

"Amelia, don't do it. It's too dangerous," said her friend Wiley Post. "I couldn't believe my ears," she later wrote. "Did Wiley Post, the man who braved every sort of hazard in his stratosphere flying, really regard a simple little flight from Mexico City to New York across the gulf as too hazardous? If so, I could scarcely wait to be on my way."

On April 19, 1935, Earhart took off from Burbank, California, bound for Mexico City. Funds for the trip were supplied by

In a 1935 newspaper cartoon, America's "flying sweetheart" shows the boys how it's done. The "fellers" include celebrated fliers Charles Lindbergh, Wiley Post, and Bernt Balchen.

780 autographed, stamped letters, carried on the flight and sold in advance by Putnam to dealers all over the world. Fifty miles short of Mexico City she landed in an arid pasture, uncertain of where she was. After astonished peasant farmers directed her in sign language, she zigzagged happily between cactus and prickly pear plants, took off, and flew on to the capital. There, President Lázaro Cárdenas and George Putnam waited to welcome her.

After a series of banquets and parties in Mexico, Earhart took off for Newark, 2,185 miles away. She arrived on Wednesday, May 8, 14 hours and 19 minutes after leaving Mexico. In Newark she was mobbed by a crowd of almost hysterical admirers. Two burly policemen came to her rescue but, she reported, "the armholder started to go one way while he who clasped my leg set out in the opposite direction. The result provided the victim with a fleeting taste of the tortures of the rack. But at that, it was fine to be home again."

Earhart, as usual, did not stay still for long. Before the month was out she had lectured in Chicago, Washington, Atlanta, New York, Indianapolis, and Muncie, Indiana. What, the press asked, would "Lady Lindy" do next? Earhart wouldn't say, but she had plans.

Now completely confident of her abilities as a pilot, she was determined to prove to the world that women were no longer second-class citizens, but potentially bold and courageous leaders. In the spring of 1935 she started to consider a "hop" that would outdo anything she—or any other pilot—had ever done. She was thinking of flying around the world.

Writing about her flight over the Gulf of Mexico, Earhart had written: "I promised my lovely red Vega I'd fly her across no more water. And I promised myself that any further over-ocean flying would be attempted in a plane with more than one motor, capable of keeping aloft with a single engine. Just in case.

"Which, in a way, was for me the beginning of the world flight project. Where to find the tree on which costly airplanes grow, I did not know."

Asked by reporters how she feels about her new Lockheed Electra, Earhart obligingly — and sincerely — demonstrates her sentiments about the big silver plane.

NINE

Around the World

In June 1935 Earhart accepted a part-time position at Purdue University in Lafayette, Indiana. She agreed to spend one month each year on campus, serving as aeronautical adviser and women's career counselor. Earhart considered Purdue, 1,000 of whose 6,000 students were women, an exciting and progressive institution. It had a growing aviation department, and had even built its own airport.

Slender, energetic, breezy in manner and dress, Earhart seemed to the students more like one of themselves than an internationally celebrated, 38-year-old aviator and businesswoman. She gave talks, answered nonstop questions about the world of aviation and her own part in it, and made herself available for late-night chats with students. Her conviction that women not only could, but should, free themselves from their traditional, "feminine" roles made her especially admired by the women at Purdue.

In addition to working with the university's faculty and undergraduates, Earhart continued with her hectic schedule of speechmaking and business meetings with Transcontinental Air. In June another painful bout with her chronic sinusitis brought her to a Los Angeles hospital for further surgery on her nasal passages. This time, her convalescence was complicated by severe chest and back pains, which were soon diagnosed as pleurisy, an inflammation of the lining of the lungs.

Earhart's impatience with her own illnesses usually resulted in surprisingly speedy recoveries, and this occasion was no different. She was spending long days at Burbank airport, polishing her flying skills and discussing aviation with Paul Mantz and the other pilots who made the airport their informal clubhouse. The topic that most interested the fliers was the Arctic Circle flight then being planned by Earhart's good friend Wiley Post. The celebrated pilot was to be accompanied by Will Rogers, another of Earhart's close friends. (Rogers, a hugely popular humorist, is perhaps best remembered for his line, "I never met a man I didn't like.")

On August 11 Earhart, Putnam, and Post were guests at Will Rogers' ranch in Santa Monica. Four days later Post and

Rogers were killed when their plane crashed in a dense fog over Alaska. Like their admirers all over the world, Earhart was shocked and deeply grieved by the tragedy. It made her even more determined, however, to press on with her own round-the-world plans. The route she had chosen would be longer and more hazardous than the one Post had planned to fly. She would circle the globe at the equator, a distance of 25,000 miles.

A few weeks after Post and Rogers' crash, Earhart competed in the Los Angeles-to-Cleveland Bendix race. She knew that her Vega, far slower than most of the other entrants' planes, had no chance of winning, but Mantz advised her to make the race for practice, estimating that she might come in fifth. He was correct; Earhart, flying with Mantz as a passenger, was fifth. "We cranked up and cruised along and won $500," she said in a letter to her mother. "Enough to pay our expenses. We had fun. Old Bessie the fire horse came through."

Earhart and Mantz had become a solid team; every hour she could spare from the lecture circuit she spent with him, doggedly practicing instrument, or "blind," flying. Air time was not easy to find; in 1935 Earhart made 136 speeches to a total of 80,000 people.

In April 1936 Purdue announced it had raised $50,000 to purchase a "flying laboratory" for its aeronautical adviser, Amelia Earhart. University officials said the aircraft—a Lockheed Electra—would be used to learn more about such crucial matters as the effect of altitude on the human body.

The press immediately began to ask questions: Was Earhart planning a new flight? Did she expect to circle the globe? If so, when? Earhart, who saw no point in alerting the public before her plans were more definite, denied any such prospect. Meanwhile, Putnam was quietly rallying political and financial support for the flight, appealing both to private investors and large airline corporations. He asked Eleanor Roosevelt to arrange for assistance from the State Department, requesting that she maintain strict secrecy about Earhart's new venture.

On July 22 Earhart flew the new Electra for the first time; both she and Mantz were delighted with the sleek, silver plane. The latest Lockheed design, it was equipped with the most sophisticated instruments available. It carried a two-way radio and extra fuel tanks that would allow nonstop flights as long as 4,500 miles.

Anxious to put the new machine to work, Earhart once again entered the Bendix race, this time making the run from New York to Los Angeles. Helen Richey, America's first female airline pilot, acted as her co-pilot. Plagued by troubles—the fuel lines clogged and a newly installed navigation hatch blew open in flight—Earhart again finished fifth. She considered the outcome a victory anyway: although most of the competitors were men, the race was won by Earhart's friends Louise Thaden and Blanche Noyes.

Two weeks after the race, Earhart told reporters that she was "nearly sold on this idea of flying around the world." But because of her busy schedule, she said, her plans were not yet complete.

Humorist Will Rogers and aviator Wiley Post relax before taking off for the Arctic circle. On August 15, 1935, Post's plane crashed in a fog in Alaska, killing both its occupants.

Earhart and Putnam spent the 1937 New Year holiday with their friends Floyd Odlum and Jacqueline Cochran. During leisurely dinners, long horseback rides, and lazy afternoons in the sun at the Odlums' California ranch, Cochran tried to talk Earhart out of her planned journey. The flight, she insisted, was not worth the danger it would entail. Fellow aviator and mutual friend Louise Thaden agreed; she even flew out to California to say so.

In her 1973 memoir, *High, Wide and Frightened*, Thaden recalled her conversation with Earhart at the ranch. "Why stick your neck out a mile on this round-the-world flight?" she had said. "You don't need to do anything more. You're tops now and if you never do anything else you always will be. It seems to me you've got everything to lose and nothing to gain."

"I've wanted to do this flight for a long time," Earhart had replied. "I've worked hard and I deserve one fling during my lifetime.... If I should pop off, it will be doing the thing I've always wanted to do."

Thaden remembered how impressed she had been by Earhart's "staunch fineness, her clear-eyed honesty, her unbiased fairness, the undefeated spirit ... the nervous reserve which has carried her through exhausting flights and more exhausting lecture tours."

Earhart listened to her friends' advice, but she was not to be dissuaded. As she wrote in *Last Flight*, "Here was my belief

Parked between Earhart and the Electra she received from Purdue is her brand-new "flivver," another gift from the university.

Earhart explains her plan to circumnavigate the planet "at its waistline." She announced the projected flight at a press conference in February 1937.

that now and then women should do for themselves what men have already done—and occasionally what men have not done—thereby establishing themselves as persons, and perhaps encouraging other women toward greater independence of thought and action. Some such consideration was a contributing reason for my wanting to do what I so much wanted to do."

Clearly, for Earhart the flight would stand as a strong statement about the real capabilities of modern women. In attempting it, she sought to wrench women out of their role as second-class citizens and place them on a level of equality with men.

At a crowded New York City press conference in February 1937, Earhart finally announced her plans for a globe-circling flight. When excited reporters asked why she wanted to make the trip, she replied, "Well, I've seen the North Atlantic, and I've seen the Pacific, too. Just say I want to fly around the globe at its waistline."

The next months were spent in extensive planning under the direction of Paul Mantz. Lockheed technicians equipped the Electra with new navigational devices, and George Putnam arranged to have expert mechanics stationed along the proposed route. As the preparations went on, Earhart continued her grueling routine of lecturing and training.

In March 1937, accompanied by Mantz and two navigators, Earhart took off for Hawaii from Oakland, California, on the first leg of the flight. They reached their destination safely, but their next takeoff, for Howland Island in the mid-Pacific, was a near-disaster.

Earhart goes over flight plans with Paul Mantz, the skillful professional pilot who had replaced Bernt Balchen as her aviation consultant.

The heavily loaded Electra moved easily down the runway until one wing dipped suddenly, sending the plane swerving crazily to the left. Earhart quickly throttled back on the left engine, which made the plane career in a wide circle. The right landing gear tore free and gas sprayed out onto the ground. Thinking fast, Earhart quickly cut the switches to prevent the plane from bursting into flames. One of the Electra's wings, both propellers, and the landing gear were badly damaged, but no one was hurt.

There were differences of opinion about the crackup. Mantz believed it was caused by Earhart's throttling back on the engine; some witnesses said the heavy plane had skidded on the wet runway, and others reported that a tire had blown out. Earhart herself thought a shock absorber had collapsed; in any case, although the mishap delayed the realization of Earhart's dream, it did not end it. "Of course the flight is still on!" she told reporters. She and the crew sailed back to California on the *Malolo* and the torn and twisted Electra went back to the Lockheed factory for repairs.

Back in Los Angeles, Lockheed technicians estimated that the extensive repairs required by the Electra would take a minimum of five weeks and cost at least $25,000. The new takeoff was scheduled for the end of May; because of seasonal weather changes, the route was entirely reversed. Earhart would fly from California to Florida to South America. From there she would cross the Atlantic Ocean and fly across Africa, India, and Southeast Asia. Then it would be down to Australia and on to the Pacific island of New Guinea. The next leg would take her over a long and perilous stretch of the uncharted south-central Pacific to tiny Howland Island. From Howland it would be

After an aborted takeoff from Honolulu's Luke field on March 20, 1937, a shaken but unhurt Earhart and Fred Noonan emerge from the cockpit of their Electra. The mishap seriously damaged the plane.

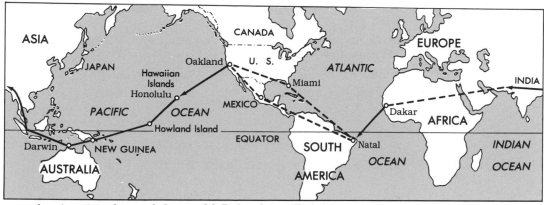

Earhart's original round-the-world flight plan called for her to head west from California. When an accident delayed the flight, her course had to be reversed because of seasonal weather changes. The new route was from west to east.

on to Honolulu and then home to Oakland.

Before the new flight could take place, a substantial sum of money had to be raised to pay for repairs and for the repositioning of fuel and mechanics along the way. Financiers Floyd Odlum and Bernard Baruch and explorer Richard Byrd were among those who advanced money for the work. Putnam and Earhart also spent most of their personal savings to pay the new expenses. "Well," she said to friends, "I'm mortgaging the future— but then, what are futures for?"

As navigator for the round-the-world flight, Earhart chose Fred Noonan, a highly skilled airman who had until recently worked for Pan American Airways. Noonan had served as chief inspector for all Pan Am bases and had mapped out the company's new Far East-Pacific routes. He was known throughout the aviation industry as a superb celestial navigator; he was, however, also known as an alcoholic. By the time Earhart signed him on for her 1937 global flight,

he had been fired by Pan Am and was considered unemployable by almost everyone in the field of aviation.

Alcoholics were nothing new to Earhart. She had dealt with the problem in her father, and in Bill Stultz, the pilot who had flown her across the Atlantic in 1928. She was sure she could handle Noonan. He promised her he would stay sober during the flight, and she had faith in his word.

As the departure date drew nearer, Paul Mantz grew increasingly worried. Mantz liked and respected Earhart and had great faith in her abilities. Her personal safety was uppermost in his mind. But George Putnam, he thought, was moving things along too quickly, advising Earhart to spend too much time on fundraising and personal appearances and too little time on preparing for the flight.

Mantz's fears were magnified when he learned that Earhart had decided to remove the Electra's 250-foot trailing radio antenna, whose operation she considered an unnecessary annoyance. She had also ordered the removal of the plane's telegraph key, explaining that since neither she nor Noonan were familiar with Morse code, the key was simply extra weight.

Without the antenna or the telegraph key, the Electra would cross the south-central Pacific with only minimal ability to contact ground stations or ships at sea. Earhart had greatly reduced the number of people who would be able to pick up her radio messages; she had also reduced her own ability to receive messages from the ground. Safe completion of the longest and most dangerous leg of the journey would now depend heavily on Noonan's navigational skills.

Despite Mantz's profound unease, Earhart and Noonan left Miami for San Juan, Puerto Rico, at dawn on June 1, 1937. They had taken off on the first leg of the round-the-world flight. Talking to a reporter before the takeoff, Earhart said, "I have a feeling there is just about one more good flight left in my system and I hope this trip is it. Anyway, when I have fin-

Waiting for Miami airport mechanics to service her Electra, Earhart confers with her husband on May 29, 1937. Three days later, she and navigator Fred Noonan took off on their round-the-world flight.

ished this job, I mean to give up long-distance 'stunt' flying."

When the Electra was 100 miles out to sea, a Miami radio station broadcast a bulletin announcing the start of Earhart's historic flight. For the next 32 days, news of "Lady Lindy's" progress made front-page headlines around the world. Earhart's log entries, mailed to the New York *Herald Tribune* from every airport she and Noonan visited, were printed in the *Tribune* and hundreds of other newspapers, where they were avidly read by millions of people.

Along with details about the flight, Earhart sent reports on the terrains, cultures, and people she and Noonan encountered. "Beautiful in the early morning light," read one such entry, "was the curving line made where the blue depths of the Gulf Stream met the aquamarine of the shoal waters off the coast." In another entry, Earhart wrote of "varicolored tendrils of the sea" that resembled "vivid green snakes wriggling in a maritime Garden of Eden."

At Paramaribo, Dutch Guiana (now Surinam), she described clouds that dropped "to shroud the shoulders of the mountains," and wondered "how many of the earthbound realize the relative nearness of sunlight above the cloud-covering? How many know that perhaps only 3,000 feet above the gray dank world my plane, if I will it, may emerge into sunlight over a billowy sea of clouds stretching away into blue infinity?"

In Fortaleza, Brazil, Earhart noted the surprised reaction of the local residents to a woman who piloted an airplane. "I'm stared at in the streets," she wrote. "I feel

Perched on the wing of her "flying laboratory," Earhart says goodbye to her husband at Miami Municipal Airport. Moments later, her Lockheed Electra was airborne. It was June 1, 1937.

they think, 'Oh, well, she's American and they're all crazy.'" Nevertheless, the Electra's crew was warmly welcomed at all its stops. "Everywhere we go," noted Earhart, "someone steps up to offer food and shelter, baths and launderings."

On June 7 the Electra reached Senegal, on Africa's west coast, after a 1,900-mile

Preceding his skipper, navigator Fred Noonan climbs into the Electra in San Juan, Puerto Rico. From here, the pair flew to Venezuela and Brazil; the next stop would be Africa.

flight over the South Atlantic. Here Earhart was deeply impressed with the "majesty" and "innate dignity" of the nation's black citizens. "What have we in the United States," she mused, "done to these proud people, so handsome and intelligent in the setting of their own country?"

Flying in 1,000-mile "hops," Earhart and Noonan crossed the vast African continent, no simple matter, as Noonan reported to his wife. "Maps of the country," he wrote, "are very inaccurate and consequently extremely misleading.... Recognizable landmarks are few and far between, one part of the desert being as much like another as two peas in a pod."

Earhart and Noonan took off from Africa's eastern edge on June 15; 1,920 miles and 13 hours later, they landed in Karachi, India (now Karachi, Pakistan). Here the weary pair took a two-day rest while mechanics replaced engine parts and overhauled the Electra.

From Karachi, they flew to Calcutta, India, 1,390 miles away, in eight and one-half hours. Navigation was relatively simple on this leg of the trip; the Electra's charts correctly indicated the many mountains, rivers, and railroad tracks below. The weather, however, was less helpful. The monsoon season, an annual period of torrential rains and wind, was on its way, and the flight ran into a number of intense rainstorms.

Earhart and Noonan were ready to leave Calcutta for Akyab, Burma, on the morning of June 18. The airfield, drenched and muddy after an all-night rain, presented a discouraging prospect. Weather forecasts, however, predicted rain, rain and more rain, which might delay their takeoff for days.

George Putnam had organized a massive Fourth of July homecoming celebration in Oakland and it was Earhart's intention to be there. Deciding she had no time to lose, she took off. It was a tense moment. "The plane," she wrote later, "clung for what seemed like ages to the heavy, sticky soil before the wheels finally lifted, and we cleared with nothing at all to spare the fringe of trees at the airdrome's edge."

Following a hasty refueling at Akyab, the Electra was once again airborne, now bound for Rangoon, Burma's capital. On the way the plane was pounded by rough air and relentless rain. Lamented Earhart, "The monsoon, I find, lets down more liquid per second than I thought could come out of the skies. Everything was obliterated in the deluge, so savage that it beat off patches of paint along the leading edge of my plane's wings. Only a flying submarine could have prospered."

After flying through what she called "an almost unbroken wall of water," Ear-

Earhart (in plaid shirt) and Fred Noonan (back to camera) lunch with airport employees in Carípito, Venezuela, the second of 28 stops the aviators would make in their effort to circumnavigate the globe.

hart landed the Electra safely in Rangoon. From there, she took the plane to Bangkok, Siam (now Thailand), and then to the British colony of Singapore. Here she and Noonan were invited to stay with the American consul and his wife. "They had courage enough," noted Earhart with appreciative humor, "to take us for the night, even after I explained our disagreeable habit of getting up at three in the morning and falling asleep immediately after dinner."

From Singapore Earhart headed for Australia, making three stops on the way. In Bandung, Indonesia, she placed a telephone call to Putnam as she waited for mechanics to make minor repairs on the Electra. When she got through to her husband in the United States, Earhart's first words were, "He's hitting the bottle again and I don't even know where he's getting it!" The "he," of course, was Noonan.

Chafing under Earhart's command, exhausted by her relentless demands for long, often frightening, "hops," Noonan had broken his word about drinking. His alcohol consumption had, in fact, been steadily increasing ever since he and Earhart had left South America. Unable to put a stop to it, Earhart had been taking on more and more of the navigation herself; from this point until they reached home, it looked as though most of the navigating would be done by the pilot.

Earhart and Noonan landed in Darwin, Australia, on June 27. Three days later they arrived in Lae, New Guinea, where Earhart wrote in her logbook, "Twenty-two thousand miles have been covered so far. There are 7,000 more to go." Her itinerary called for two more landings between Lae and Oakland, California: one at Howland Island, 2,556 miles from Lae, the next at Honolulu, Hawaii, 1,900 miles from Howland. The last leg of the journey, from Hawaii to Oakland, was 2,400 miles.

By far the most dangerous stretch was the one between Lae and Howland. Finding the island, which was virtually a pinprick in the middle of the immense Pacific Ocean, would require the most precise navigational skills of the entire trip.

On Howland Island preparations for the Electra's arrival were complete. A new runway had been built and government officials were standing by. The U.S. Coast Guard cutter *Itasca* was lying off the shore and the cutter *Ontario* was stationed at sea midway between Lae and Howland. The *Itasca* was responsible for sending the radio signals that would guide the Electra to Howland.

In her last log entry Earhart wrote: "Not much more than a month ago I was on the other shore of the Pacific, looking westward. This evening, I look eastward over the Pacific. In those fast-moving days which have intervened, the whole width of the world has passed behind us—except this broad ocean. I shall be glad when we have the hazards of its navigation behind us."

In the final hours before Earhart took off for Howland, confusion surrounded the question of radio transmission between the Electra, the weather station at Lae, and the Coast Guard vessels stationed in the Pacific. Commander Warner Thompson of the *Itasca* later commented, "Viewed from the fact that Miss Earhart's flight was largely dependent upon radio communication, her attitude toward arrangements was most casual, to say the least."

The *Itasca*'s radio crew had advised Earhart to transmit on one frequency and she wired back her intent to transmit on another. Personnel on the ship did not know the trailing antenna had been removed; nor were they aware that neither Earhart nor Noonan knew Morse code. Before the situation could be cleared up, Earhart was off. It was 10 o'clock on the morning of July 2.

Noonan had spent the previous evening drinking with friends and complaining about Earhart's exacting schedule. The morning of their departure from Lae was like a replay of the scene with Stultz at Trepassey airport nine years earlier; Noonan had a massive hangover and had

As Earhart's Electra roared through the skies, millions of people all over the world followed newspaper and radio reports of its progress.

to be helped into the Electra's cockpit.

Loaded with 1,150 gallons of gasoline, the Electra was difficult to maneuver and Earhart had trouble getting into the air. Local pilots held their breath as the plane reached the end of the jungle runway and headed over the ocean, its propellers hitting the tops of the waves. Earhart finally brought the nose of the plane up; as the onlookers cheered, it climbed into the Pacific sky and out of sight.

One of the watching pilots later said that he and the other fliers who had flown Lockheed aircraft "were loud in their praise of the takeoff with such an over-load." Back in California, Earhart's mother heard the news on the radio. Her daughter's takeoff was described as "a thrilling one, with the large plane getting into the air with only 50 yards of runway to spare. Even now," continued the announcer's voice, "her huge plane is roaring over the South Pacific." Pointed straight at Howland Island, the Electra was expected there 18 hours later.

After she had been in the air for 7 hours and 20 minutes—about one-third of the way to Howland—Earhart called the Lae radio station. She said she was flying at 7,000 feet, dead on course, and that she was switching to another frequency for the night. The Lae radio operator told her that her signal was clear, and urged her to remain on the same frequency. Perhaps Earhart did not hear the request; perhaps she decided to pay no attention to it. In any case, she switched her frequency. The dialogue was the last two-way communication the Electra would ever have with anyone.

Almost 2,000 miles away, in the calm waters off Howland Island, Thompson and his crew of radio experts on the *Itasca* were waiting to guide the Electra to a safe landing. It was going to be a long night. At 2:45 A.M. Howland Island time, when Earhart had been aloft for more than 14 hours, her voice drifted in, clouded by static. She gave her radio call letters and the weather: "KHAQQ ... cloudy ... weather cloudy." The men on the *Itasca* strained to hear more, but that was the end of the transmission.

Between 2:45 and 6:15 A.M. the *Itasca* heard two faint, short transmissions from Earhart. Each time, the ship's radio operators responded immediately, both with Morse code and voice, "What is your position? When do you expect to arrive at Howland?"

There was no response.

Noonan had estimated the Electra's ar-

Tiny Howland Island, the next-to-last scheduled stop on Earhart and Noonan's round-the-world flight, awaits the arrival of the fliers on July 3, 1937. They never appeared.

rival time at Howland at 6:30 A.M. At 6:15, Earhart's voice came over loud and clear. She asked for a radio bearing, and said she would whistle into the microphone to allow the *Itasca* to get a fix on her position. The ship's radio operator heard a sound that might have been a whistle, but it was too brief to allow him to get a bearing. He asked her to repeat the sound, but he got no reply.

A new weather report indicated heavy clouds and rain squalls northwest of Howland; Earhart, the men of the *Itasca* knew, must have already run into it. Suddenly, they heard her again: "Give me the weather!" she said. "I've got to know the weather!"

The radio operator responded immediately, transmitting the information on all available channels. Again, there was only silence from the Electra.

As the sun rose, the *Itasca* was sending a continuous homing signal to Earhart. Tension aboard the ship was almost unbearable. At 6:45 Earhart, sounding exhausted, was back on the air: "Please take a bearing on us and report in half an hour. I will make a noise in microphone. About 100 miles out. Position doubtful." Once again, she did not stay in contact

long enough for the *Itasca* to locate her.

At 7:42 there was another message from Earhart. This time, her voice was crisp and distinct. "We must be on you but cannot see you. But gas is running low. Have been unable to reach you by radio. We are flying at 1,000 feet."

On deck the *Itasca*'s crew frantically scanned the sky; the Electra should be visible by now. They saw nothing. Earhart did not acknowledge their response to her call.

During the next hour, Earhart's voice was heard twice, but she was still apparently unable to hear the signals from the ship, and the ship was still unable to fix her position. She was now more than two hours overdue. At 8:45 she came through again. The desperately worried Coast Guardsmen leaned close to their radio and heard Earhart's voice, now sounding almost panicked: "We are on the line of position 157-337," she said. She concluded her cryptic message with the words, "We are running north and south."

The transmission was followed by silence. The world never heard Amelia Earhart's voice again. Along with Fred Noonan, she had vanished.

Amelia Earhart flew many types of aircraft during her 17-year flying career. She loved them all, but one had a special place in her heart — the Lockheed Vega that had carried her across the Atlantic Ocean in 1932.

TEN

Earhart's Legacy

The world received the news of Earhart's disappearance with stunned disbelief. Newspapers had stressed the near impossibility of finding an island that was a mere pinpoint in a vast ocean, but the public had been sure that "Lady Lindy" would find her way.

The search for the Electra began soon after Earhart's last radio transmission, at 8:45 A.M. on July 3, 1937. The *Itasca* continued to produce the towering plume of black smoke with which its officers had hoped to guide Earhart to Howland Island. Then, without any clear idea of where to start, the cutter headed northwest into the stormy area where the Electra might have gone down. When word of the missing plane reached the mainland, a huge task force was assembled, forming one of the largest search parties in history. Included in the force were 60 planes and 10 ships, among them the aircraft carrier *Lexington* and the battleship *Colorado*. The search covered an area of 250,000 square miles, lasted two weeks, and cost $4 million. It found nothing.

Theories about Earhart and Noonan's fate sprang up almost at once. The most

logical guess was that the fliers had gotten lost, run out of gas, and gone down in the Pacific. In 1937, however, many people were convinced that war between Japan and the United States was imminent. That conviction led to widespread rumors that Earhart had been on a spy mission over the Japanese-held Pacific Islands, instructed by the White House to photograph Japanese military installations. A large body of serious researchers insist to this day that Earhart and Noonan crash-landed on some small island, were captured by the Japanese, mistaken for spies, and executed or held in prison until their deaths.

Another common theory held that the Electra's disappearance had been staged in order to allow the U.S. Navy a chance to conduct a search in the South Pacific. Earhart's otherwise inexplicable problems with her radio communications were seen as a deliberate tactic.

Both the U.S. Navy and the distraught George Putnam requested permission from the Japanese to search the waters around the Japanese-ruled Pacific islands. Japanese diplomats responded

Earhart and Noonan's Electra already overdue, George Putnam and Mary Noonan tensely scan the latest bulletins from the Pacific on July 3, 1937.

pers and magazines continue to appear in the 1980s. It is unlikely that the public's curiosity about Amelia Earhart will ever be satisfied.

Amy Earhart continued to hope that her daughter would return. For years she kept a suitcase packed with toilet articles, sunburn cream, and a pair of scissors to cut her daughter's hair. Each evening at dusk she stood on the balcony of her Los Angeles apartment and gazed out over the Pacific, expecting to see the shining silver Electra come over the horizon at any moment.

In a newspaper interview 20 years after her daughter's disappearance, Amy Earhart said she was now convinced that Amelia had been on a mission for the U.S. government, and that she had been captured by the Japanese, taken to Tokyo, and killed. Known as "Mother Earhart" to countless young women who idolized her daughter, Amy Earhart died in 1962.

The riddle of Earhart's final days is intriguing. Even more exciting, however, is the triumph of her life. Earhart had been many things—premedical student, nurse's aide, social worker, lecturer, writer, editor, feminist—but first and foremost, she was an individualist. Flying was the passion of her life; she never even considered bowing to the conventions of the day by marrying, "settling down," and giving up aviation.

Earhart was not the only woman to take to the skies in the 1920s, nor was she the only woman to speak up for the rights of her sex. But she was the most celebrated of these pioneers, and she used her celebrity to advance the causes she believed in. An instant star after she be-

with the polite assurance that they would themselves conduct a thorough search. They reported no trace of the fliers.

"Earhart fever" raged throughout the world. Newspapers picked up a story about a New Jersey woman said to be Earhart in disguise, or Earhart with amnesia. Another rumor had Earhart living on a South Pacific island as a native, married to a local fisherman. Although the "fever" has diminished with the years, it has by no means disappeared. Books, television shows, and articles in newspa-

Muriel Earhart Morrissey talks to reporters in 1970. Standing before a picture of her famous sister, Morrissey firmly denied current reports that a New Jersey housewife was really Amelia Earhart in disguise.

came the first woman to cross the Atlantic Ocean by air, Earhart spent much of the rest of her life trying to prove—largely to herself—that she was worthy of the fame and affection the world lavished on her.

Amelia Earhart was certainly not without faults: she had no hesitation in showing her scornful impatience with those who were incompetent or indecisive, and no reluctance to capitalize on her fame. A profoundly solitary person, she sometimes neglected family and friends for her obsession with flight, and she was often

American officials lay the cornerstone of the Earhart Light on Howland Island. The structure, one of many monuments to the vanished flier, was scheduled to send a beam of light across the Pacific every four seconds.

stubborn enough to insist she knew best, even when she might have benefited from the advice of others.

Although she had a normal complement of human failings, Earhart also had qualities that set her apart and made her one of the 20th century's true heroes. She made tremendous demands on herself, and she rarely failed to live up to them. Her courage was enormous, her integrity without question. Her commitment to aviation helped create an industry whose far-reaching benefits have improved the lives of millions of people. She was determined to prove that women were capable of accomplishing at least as much as men. That determination led a generation of women to seek new horizons and new roles for themselves.

Earhart's disappearance prompted a flood of speeches and words of praise. Perhaps none were more eloquent than those spoken by her friend and fellow aviator, Jacqueline Cochran. "If her last flight was into eternity," said Cochran, "Amelia did not lose, for her last flight was endless. Like in a relay race of progress, she had merely placed the torch in the hands of others to carry on to the next goal and from there on and forever."

The story of Earhart's death remains a mystery. The story of her life, however, is a clear testament to courage and its rewards. She blazed a trail that countless others — both men and women — will continue to follow.

FURTHER READING

Backus, Jean L. *Letters from Amelia.* Boston: Beacon Press, 1982.

Briand, Paul L., Jr. *Daughter of the Sky.* New York: Duell, Sloan and Pearce, 1960.

Burke, John. *Winged Legend.* New York: G.P. Putnam's Sons, 1970.

Earhart, Amelia. *The Fun of It.* Chicago: Academy Press, Ltd., 1977.

———. *Last Flight* (arranged by George Palmer Putnam). New York: Harcourt, Brace & Company, 1937.

———. *20 Hrs. 40 Min.* New York: G.P. Putnam's Sons, 1928.

Lindbergh, Anne Morrow. *Hour of Gold, Hour of Lead.* New York: Harcourt Brace Jovanovich, 1973.

Loomis, Vincent V., and Jeffrey L. Ethell. *Amelia Earhart: The Final Story.* New York: Random House, 1985.

Moolman, Valerie. *Women Aloft.* Alexandria, VA: Time-Life Books, 1981.

Morrissey, Muriel Earhart. *Courage Is the Price.* Wichita, KS: McCormick-Armstrong Publishing Division, 1963.

Putnam, George Palmer. *Soaring Wings.* New York: Harcourt, Brace & Company, 1939.

Strippel, Dick. *Amelia Earhart: The Myth and the Reality.* Jericho, NY: Exposition Press, 1972.

Thaden, Louise. *High, Wide and Frightened.* New York: Air Facts Press, 1973.

CHRONOLOGY

July 24, 1897	Born Amelia Mary Earhart in Atchison, Kansas
Sept. 1916	Enters the Ogontz School near Philadelphia
1918	Serves as a nurse's aide at Spadina Military Hospital in Toronto, Canada
1919	Enrolls as a premedical student at Columbia University
1920–22	Moves to Los Angeles and begins flying lessons
1922	Receives pilot's license and buys first airplane
Oct. 1922	Sets women's altitude record at a Los Angeles, California, airshow
1926–28	Takes job as a social worker at Denison House in Boston
June 18, 1928	As a passenger, becomes the first woman to fly across the Atlantic Ocean
Sept. 1928	Publishes *20 Hrs. 40 Min.*
	Becomes first woman to fly round trip across the United States solo
1929	Comes in third in the Women's Air Derby
	Elected first president of an all-female aviation society, the Ninety-Nines
Feb. 7, 1931	Marries publisher/manager George Palmer Putnam
May 21, 1932	Becomes first woman to fly the Atlantic Ocean solo
1932	Awarded France's Cross of the Legion of Honor and the National Geographic Society's Special Gold Medal; becomes the first woman to receive the U.S. Distinguished Flying Cross
	Publishes *The Fun of It*
Jan. 12, 1935	Becomes the first person to fly from Hawaii to California and the first to solo anywhere over the Pacific Ocean
May 1935	Becomes the first person to solo from Burbank, California, to Mexico City and from Mexico City to Newark, New Jersey
1935–36	Works as an aeronautical adviser and career counselor at Purdue University
June 1, 1937	Embarks on a round-the-world flight
July 3, 1937	Loses radio contact with ground support crews en route from New Guinea to Howland Island; disappears

INDEX

Africa, 90, 93–94

Akyab, 95

Alaska, 84

Arizona, 64

Armour Heights, 32

Astor, Nancy, 18, 57

Atchison, 21, 22, 23

Atlanta, 81

Atlantic Ocean, 13, 16, 17, 49, 50, 55, 71, 90, 94, 103

Australia, 90, 95, 96

Backus, Jean, 29, 38

Balchen, Bernt, 14, 74

Bandung, 95

Bangkok, 95

Baruch, Bernard, 91

Boston, 43, 44, 50, 51, 52

Brazil, 93

British Guild of Airpilots and Navigators, 71

British Institute of Journalists, 71

Burbank, 81, 83

Burma, 95

Burry Port, 55

Byrd, Richard E., 49, 50, 51, 91

Calcutta, 94, 95

California, 37, 60, 63, 65, 74, 75, 77, 79, 86, 89, 90, 96, 97

Canada, 29, 30

Cárdenas, Lázaro, 81

Chapman, Samuel, 37, 40, 44, 45, 50, 66

Chicago, 26, 27, 81

Christian X, king of Belgium, 71

Churchill, Winston, 57

Cleveland, 64

Cochran, Jacqueline, 74, 86, 104

Colorado, 101

Columbia University, 34–35, 43

Columbus, 64

Connecticut, 66

Coolidge, Calvin, 57

Cosmopolitan, 60, 61

"Courage," 45

Courage Is The Price (Muriel Earhart), 26

Crosson, Marvel, 63, 64

Curtiss School of Aviation, 39

Darwin, 96

Daughters of the American Revolution, 69

Denison House, 43, 44, 45, 47, 50, 60

Des Moines, 25

Dutch Guiana *see* Surinam

Earhart, Amelia Mary
  author, 24, 32, 39, 49, 52, 60, 61, 67, 72, 86
  awarded Distinguished Flying Cross, 72
  birth, 21, 22
  disappearance, 99, 101, 102
  early years, 21, 23, 24, 25, 26
  education, 26, 27, 29, 30, 33, 34, 35
  father's alcoholism and, 25, 26
  feminist, 67, 68, 72, 89, 102, 104
  learns aviation, 38, 39, 40
  on lecture circuit, 60, 61, 66
  marriage, 66
  nurse's aide, 31, 32
  president of Ninety-Nines, 64
  receives pilot's license, 41
  social worker, 43, 44, 45
  solo transatlantic flight, 13–19, 71
  solo transpacific flight, 74, 75, 77
  suffers from sinusitis, 32–33, 43, 83

world flight, 81, 84, 86, 89, 92–99
Earhart, Amy Otis (mother), 21, 22, 23, 24, 25, 26, 29, 33, 34, 35, 37, 40, 43, 52, 66, 102
Earhart, David (grandfather), 22
Earhart, Edwin (father), 22, 23, 24, 25, 26, 33, 35, 37, 41, 43, 55
Earhart, Mary (grandmother), 22
Earhart, Muriel (sister), 23, 24, 25, 26, 29, 33, 43, 65
Edward VIII, king of Great Britain, 57
England, 18, 52, 57, 71
Fairbanks, Douglas, 74
Fédération Aéronautique Internationale, 41
Florida, 90
Fortaleza, 93
Friendship, 49, 50, 51, 52, 55, 57, 60
Fun of It, The, 24, 49, 52, 67, 72
George V, king of Great Britain, 18
Gordon, Louis "Slim," 51, 52, 58, 59
Great Britain, 18, 49, 55
Guest, Amy, 49
Halifax, 52
Harbour Grace, 13, 14
Harvard University, 43
Hawaii, 73, 74, 75, 89, 96
Heath, Mary, 58
Herald Tribune, 93
High, Wide and Frightened (Thaden), 86
Honolulu, 74, 75, 91, 96
Hoover, Herbert, 19, 71, 72
Hour of Gold, Hour of Lead (Anne Lindbergh), 63
Howland Island, 89, 90, 96, 97, 98, 99, 101
Hughes, Charles Evans, 71
Hyde Park High School, 26
Ile de France, 71
India, 90, 94
Indiana, 81, 83
Indianapolis, 81
Indonesia, 95

Iowa, 25
Ireland, 17, 18, 71
Itasca, 96, 99, 101
Japan, 101, 102
Kansas, 21, 22
Kansas City, 22, 26, 29, 33
Karachi, 94
Kentucky, 65
Kimball, James "Doc," 14, 52, 65
Kinner, W. G., 41, 47
Kitty Hawk, 13
"Lady Lindy" *see* Earhart, Amelia Mary
Lae, 96, 97, 98
Lafayette, 83
Lake George, 33
Last Flight, 32, 39, 86
Layman, David T., 49
Letters from Amelia (Backus), 29, 38
Lexington, 101
Lindbergh, Anne, 63
Lindbergh, Charles, 13, 50, 57, 61, 63
London, 18, 55, 57, 71
Londonderry, 17, 71
Los Angeles, 13, 33, 35, 37, 38, 41, 60, 72, 79, 83, 84, 90
Louisville, 65
Lurline, 74
Malolo, 90
Mantz, Paul, 74, 75, 83, 84, 89, 90, 91, 92
Massachusetts, 33, 37, 74
Medford, 43, 44, 52
Mellon, Andrew, 18
Mexico, 79, 81
Mexico City, 79, 81
Miami, 92, 93
Minnesota, 26
Missouri, 26
Morrissey, Albert, 44
Muncie, 81
National Aeronautic Association, 47
National Geographic Society, 19, 72
New Guinea, 90, 96
New Jersey, 14, 72, 79

New York City, 13, 15, 34, 35, 49, 59, 60, 65, 79, 81, 84, 89
Newark, 72, 79, 81
Newfoundland, 13, 14, 16, 51
Nichols, Ruth, 41, 47, 49, 63, 64, 65
Ninety-Nines, 64
Noonan, Fred, 91, 92, 93, 94, 95, 96, 98, 99, 101
North Carolina, 13
North Hollywood, 74
Northampton, 33
Nova Scotia, 52
Noyes, Blanche, 84
Oakland, 77, 89, 91, 95, 96
Odlum, Floyd, 74, 86, 91
O'Donnell, Gladys, 63, 64
Ogontz School, 29, 30, 31
Ohio, 64
Ontario, 96
Otis, Alfred (grandfather), 21, 22
Otis, Amelia Harres (grandmother), 21, 23, 25
Otis, Amy see Earhart, Amy Otis
Otis, James, 21
Pacific Ocean, 74, 75, 77, 89, 90, 92, 96, 97, 101
Paramaribo, 94
Paris, 71
Perkins, Marion, 43, 47, 49
Philadelphia, 17, 18, 22, 29, 30, 34
Phipps, John, 49
Pickford, Mary, 74
Pius XI, 71
Post, Wiley, 74, 79, 83, 84
President Pierce, 77
President Roosevelt, 58, 59
Puerto Rico, 92
Purdue University, 83, 84
Putnam, George Palmer (husband), 14, 49, 50, 52, 60, 61, 65, 66, 67, 69, 71, 72, 74, 75, 81, 83, 84, 86, 89, 91, 95, 101
Railey, Hilton, 49, 57

Rangoon, 95
Richey, Helen, 84
Rogers, Will, 74, 83, 84
Rome, 71
Roosevelt, Eleanor, 72, 73, 84
Roosevelt, Franklin, 72
Rye, 60
St. Margaret's College, 29
San Francisco, 77
San Juan, 92
Santa Monica, 63, 64, 83
Senegal, 93
Siam see Thailand
Singapore, 95
Skyward (Byrd), 50
Smith College, 33
Snook, Neta, 39
South Pole, 14
Southampton, 57
Spadina Military Hospital, 31
Stultz, Wilmer "Bill," 51, 52, 53, 55, 57, 58, 59, 91, 96
"stunting," 39
Surinam, 93
Sutherland, Abby, 29
Teterboro Airport, 14
Thaden, Louise, 63, 64, 84, 96
Thailand, 95
Thompson, Warner, 96, 98
Tokyo, 102
Toronto, 29, 30, 31, 32, 37
Transcontinental Air Transport, 61, 65, 83
Trepassey, 51, 52, 96
20 Hrs. 40 Min., 60, 61, 72
Ulm, Charles, 75
University of Kansas, 22
Wales, 55
Washington, D.C., 69, 71, 72, 81
We (Charles Lindbergh), 50
Women's Air Derby, 63, 64, 65
World War I, 30, 39
Wright, Orville, 13
Wright, Wilbur, 13

PICTURE CREDITS

Nancy Shore holds a B.A. in English Literature from New York University. A former drama critic and feature writer for the *Providence Journal-Bulletin* and *Stages Magazine,* Shore has been staff editor at The Janet Wilkens Manus Agency and Lisa Collier Associates in New York City. Her articles have appeared in *Afternoon TV* and *Art & Artists.*

❖   ❖   ❖

Matina S. Horner is president of Radcliffe College and associate professor of psychology and social relations at Harvard University. She is best known for her studies of women's motivation, achievement, and personality development. Dr. Horner serves on several national boards and advisory councils, including those of the National Science Foundation, Time Inc., and the Women's Research and Education Institute. She earned her B. A. from Bryn Mawr College and Ph.D. from the University of Michigan, and holds honorary degrees from many colleges and universities, including Mount Holyoke, Smith, Tufts, and the University of Pennsylvania.